Nathaniel Lyon

The Last Political Writings of Gen. Nathaniel Lyon, USA

With a Sketch of his Life and Military Service

Nathaniel Lyon

The Last Political Writings of Gen. Nathaniel Lyon, USA
With a Sketch of his Life and Military Service

ISBN/EAN: 9783337058388

Printed in Europe, USA, Canada, Australia, Japan

Cover: Foto ©ninafisch / pixelio.de

More available books at **www.hansebooks.com**

THE LAST POLITICAL WRITINGS

OF

GEN. NATHANIEL LYON,

U. S. A.

WITH A

SKETCH OF HIS LIFE AND MILITARY SERVICES.

> "*I'll make thee famous by my pen,
> And glorious by my sword.*"
> GRAHAM, MARQUIS OF MONTROSE.

NEW YORK:
RUDD & CARLETON, 130 GRAND STREET.
M DCCC LXI.

TO THE PEOPLE

OF THE UNITED STATES OF AMERICA,

THESE

THE LAST WISE AND NOBLE WRITINGS

OF

GENERAL NATHANIEL LYON, U.S.A.,

THE GALLANT COMMANDER, THE HERO, AND THE PATRIOT,

WHO,

IN THE DARKEST HOUR

OF THE MONSTER REBELLION OF 1861,

SACRIFICED HIS LIFE IN DEFENCE

OF THEIR LAWS, LIBERTY, AND HONOR,

ARE DEDICATED

BY THE PUBLISHERS.

ODE,

WRITTEN IN THE BEGINNING OF THE YEAR 1746.

How sleep the brave, who sink to rest,
By all their country's wishes bless'd!
When Spring, with dewy fingers cold,
Returns to deck their hallow'd mould,
She there shall dress a sweeter sod
Than Fancy's feet have ever trod.

By fairy hands their knell is rung;
By forms unseen their dirge is sung;
There Honour comes, a pilgrim gray,
To bless the turf that wraps their clay;
And Freedom shall awhile repair,
To dwell a weeping hermit there!

WILLIAM COLLINS.

CONTENTS.

Memoir of Nathaniel Lyon,	11
Our Cause—Our Candidate,	111
Sovereign Squattereignity,	120
Are We Subdued?	135
The Moral of the Question,	139
True to His Mission,	151
Fitness for the Presidency,	161
The Secret of it,	167
Our Grievances,	176
Disunion,	184
Our Political Summary,	190
A Word to the Brethren,	194
Republican Reflections,	200
Our Triumph,	204
Proposed Amendments to the Constitution,	210
Letter I,	214
Letter II,	224
Personal Reminiscences, etc.,	233
Funeral Obsequies,	239
In Memory of General Lyon,	271
Lyon,	273

MEMOIR.

MEMOIR OF NATHANIEL LYON.

NATHANIEL LYON was born at Ashford, Windham co., Connecticut, on the — of July, 1819. He was the son of Amasa Lyon, a well-to-do farmer, for many years a magistrate, and prominent man in Ashford. His mother, whose name was Kezia, belonged to the Knowlton family. Two members of this family, Thomas and Daniel, were distinguished in the Revolution, and possibly before, for they both served in the wars of the Colonists and the English against the French, probably under Putnam, who was appointed to the command of the first troops raised in Connecticut in

1755, and who, by the way, might almost be considered a neighbor of theirs, Pomfret, his residence, being only a few miles distant from Ashford. The former of the brothers, Thomas, is well known to the readers of American History, in connexion with the battle of Bunker's Hill, where, as a Captain, he played an important part, commanding the Connecticut troops at a breastwork of hay, which he extemporized along an old rail-fence, and which formed a valuable defence to the provincials before the battle was over.

After the lapse of little more than a year, we hear of him again, as Colonel Knowlton. It was the 16th of September, 1776, and a British force, under Brigadier Leslie, was making its way by M'Gowan's pass to Harlem Plains. "The little garrisons," says Lossing, in his *Field Book of the Revolution*, "at Mount Morris and Harlem Cove (Manhattanville) confronted them at the mouth of a deep gorge, and kept them in partial check until the arrival of re-enforcements. Washington was at Morris's house, and hearing the firing, rode to his outpost, where the Convent of the Sacred Heart now stands. There he met Colonel Knowlton of the Connecticut Rangers ("*Congress's Own*,") who had been skirmishing with the advancing foe, and now came for orders. The enemy were about three hundred strong upon the plain, and had a reserve in the woods upon the heights. Knowlton was ordered to hasten with his Rangers, and Major Leitch with three companies of Weedon's Virginia regiment, to gain the rear of the advance, while a feigned attack was to be made in front. Perceiving this, the enemy rushed forward to gain an advantageous position on the plain, when they were attacked by Knowlton and Leitch on the flank. Re-enforcements now came down from the hills, when the enemy changed front, and fell upon the Americans. A short but severe conflict ensued. Three bullets passed through the body of Leitch, and he was borne away. A few minutes afterwards, Knowlton received a bullet through the head, fell, and was borne off by his sorrowing companions." So ended the battle of Harlem Plains, as far as Thomas Knowlton was concerned; for he was carried, Lossing tells us, to the redoubt, near the Hudson, at One Hundred and Fifty-Sixth street, where he expired before sunset, and was buried within the embankments. Washington honored his memory in general orders on the morning after the battle, for, alluding to his death, he wrote: "He would have been an honor to any country." This was a noble tribute, and not the last which the Knowltons were destined to receive, their valor and glory flowering again in the person of their descendant, Nathaniel Lyon.

If there be anything in ancestry (a mooted point about which the wisest differ), the boy Nathaniel was fortunate in his birth. Of his early years we have no account. They were probably passed like those of most New England children—evenly, simply, monotonously; among his brothers and sisters at home, playing, or doing childish "chores;" or at the village school, trying to realize the truth of the old proverb (which, by the way, is not particularly evident), that "Learning is better than houses and land;" floundering in the dismal, and seemingly bottomless, quagmire, which the wise call Spelling; wandering in the thorny labyrinths of Grammar; poring over the configurations of Geography, occasionally "bounding" a distant State by way of refreshing his memory; or clumsily stumbling through the delicate mysteries of pothooks and hangers! This, and more of the same sort—pictures of juvenile life in the country; groups of tanned and noisy boys, behind the school-house, along the road, or in the fields, trundling hoops, flying kites, or playing ball; roaming in the woods for birds' nests, or gathering berries in distant pastures; we can imagine all this, and be pretty sure, too, that we are not far from the truth. Still, this is not the way in which Biography ought to be written; so we will leave the unsubstantial though poetical region of Fancy, for the solid and prosaic world of Fact. Of the childhood of General Lyon, then, we know nothing, except that it was passed in his native village, and, for the most part, in the house in which he was born. This house, the homestead of the family, stands about four miles from Eastford (Ashford was divided in 1847, and the name of the northern portion of the township changed to Eastford), on the road to Hampton. Leaving the little hamlet of Phœnixville we climb a long hill, thence over a rough road to a valley, nestled in which, between two steep and rocky hills, about twenty rods from the highway, is the house—a small, old building, somewhat out of repair, with rusty clapboards, which were once painted red. Poor and unpicturesque as it is, it was precious in the eyes of General Lyon, whose memory delighted to dwell upon it in after years. The night before his last battle, he slept, we are told, with one of his friends, Major Scofield, between two high rocks, where he was so wedged in that it was difficult for him to stir; he made light of the inconvenience, however, as was his wont, and, his mind reverting to his early home and its surroundings, remarked that he was "born between two rocks."

"Nathaniel," said an aged man, to one who was present at the General's funeral, "Nathaniel worked for me on my farm when he was a boy. He was smart, daring, and resolute, and wonderfully attached to his mother." One likes to learn such things of a hero in his boyhood; they show that the child was the father of the man; that the courage we admire, and the glory we reverence, were the legitimate growth of a brave soul, and a tender, loving heart. In addition to the qualities already mentioned, Nathaniel is said to have shown, even in his early years, a great talent for mathematics, a circumstance which we can readily believe (though not the report that it was cultivated under the tuition of an experienced teacher, experienced teachers being so seldom included among the appointments of a farm!) as it probably determined his future career.

In his eighteenth year (according to one account, July 1st, 1837), he entered the Military Academy at West Point, where he remained till 1841, when he graduated with distinction, being the eleventh in his class. Appointed Second Lieutenant in the Second United States Infantry, his military life may be said to have commenced. We shall not trace him through his initiation, the months and years in which he was gaining an active knowledge of his profession, for the early part of his career, however arduous it may have been to himself, and useful to his country, was passed in obscurity. Let it suffice then, to say, that he served in the everglades of Florida in the latter part of the Seminole war; that he was stationed at various posts on our Western frontier; and that he went through the Mexican war, gradually rising in rank (he entered the latter as a First Lieutenant), and drawing attention to himself. He was engaged in the bombardment and capture of Vera Cruz; and at the battle of Cerro Gordo, his company was the only one that reached the crest of the hill in time to engage the Mexicans before their retreat. "No sooner had the height become ours," said Captain Morris, who commanded the regiment, "than the enemy appeared in large force on the Jalapa road, and we were ordered to hasten to that point. Captain Canby, with a small detachment, accompanied by Lieutenant Lyon, pressed hotly in their rear, and were soon in possession of a battery of three pieces which had been firing upon us in reverse."

At Contreras, Lieutenant Lyon's regiment performed an important part in resisting the onslaught of the enemy's cavalry, and his own command, held in reserve in the centre of the hollow square formed for resistance to the attack, did most signal service. And on the day after the battle, he himself, at the head of his men, followed in pursuit of the routed Mexicans, and succeeded in capturing several pieces of their artillery, which he immediately turned upon their flying forces. He also distinguished himself at Churubusco, and for his gallantry in both actions received the following recommendation in the regimental returns of his commanding officer, Acting Colonel Morris. "I here take the opportunity of recommending these two officers (Captains Casey and Wessels), together with Captain J. R. Smith and First Lieutenant Lyon, to the special notice of the Colonel commanding the brigade." The result of this honorable mention was the appointment of Lieutenant Lyon to the rank of Brevet Captain. He also assisted in the capture of the city of Mexico, and while fighting in the streets, near the Belen Gate, received a wound from a musket ball.

Peace being declared with Mexico, Captain Lyon (he received the rank of full Captain on the 11th of June, 1851) was ordered to Jefferson Barracks, Missouri, preparatory to a contemplated march overland to California. By a change of orders from the War Department, however, his regiment was dispatched by the way of Cape Horn, and arrived in California shortly after its acquisition by the United States. He remained in California for a number of years, longer, it is said, than most of his fellow officers, seeing all sorts of life and service incident to his profession in a new and partially wild country. His time was chiefly employed in fighting the Indians, an enemy not to be judged by the ordinary standard, or conquered by the ordinary means; but by long and tedious marches, sudden surprises, incessant alarms, and frequent skirmishes—in short, by a barbaric strategy similar, but superior, to their own. The schooling which he had had in the everglades of Florida was of use to him now, and he soon became proficient in this style of warfare. It was adapted to the cast of his mind, which was in many respects that of a partisan leader; not that he was deficient in the art of his profession, the science of war, for he was a thoroughly scientific soldier; but that it suited his rapid way of thinking, and prompt way of acting.

He was finally removed from California, which we will suppose became in time so far free from Indians, as no longer to need his services, and was stationed on our Western frontiers, chiefly in Kansas and Nebraska. It was at the height of the political troubles there, the history of which we all know, and the result of which we all see, in the conflicts which are now dividing our unhappy country. His position as an officer of the Government, his peculiar position, we may almost say, remembering who filled the Presidential Chair then (who so abject now as the white-haired, broken-down old man at Wheatlands?) made him acquainted with the most prominent men of that section, border ruffians and the like, and the measures which the Government were trying to force upon the people. As he had always been accustomed to think for himself, he soon began to have a very decided opinion concerning the merits of the case then and there on trial—Freedom *versus* Slavery, and it is no slander to his memory to say that it was not in favor of the latter. He was, or had been, a Democrat, but the scenes of fraud and violence with which he was surrounded, and which he could hardly fail to trace to the Democratic party, made him look for salvation in another political creed. The change which he experienced at that time, led him at a later period to enter what was to him a new field of operations—the world in which the pen and not the sword rules. The result may be seen in the articles which follow. They were written in the summer and fall of 1860, while he was stationed at Camp Riley, Kansas, and were published in a weekly paper issued in that vicinity, *The Manhattan Express*. The date of their appearance is annexed to each. The motive which impelled Captain Lyon to write these articles, was that which made him a soldier and kept him one—a sincere, earnest desire to be useful to his country. What other motive could have induced a soldier like him to lay down his sword and take up the pen, a weapon to which he was unaccustomed, and in the use of which the merest literary tyro might worst him? Not vanity, for his articles were published anonymously; and certainly not spite, for no one in power had injured him. He may have been wrong in some of his conclusions (we do not say that he was), if so, the error was that of an honest man, not a demagogue. That his heart was in his work is evident from his notes at this time. "My article is longer than I wished," he wrote to the editor on the 11th of Sept. 1860, " but it could hardly be shorter and argumentative. I have tried to show what I believe Mr. Douglas's conduct admits of—an intention, in spite of all circumstances, to do what he can for the pro-slavery party, and his pretended opposition is only to be able to serve them better. I may not have made this as plain as I had wished and intended, but must let it pass now."

"I have not been able to write you for this week's paper," he wrote again on the 23d Nov., "and have been under the impression that you would not expect me to do so.

"There seems to be little doubt that several of the Southern States will precipitate themselves into disaster and disgrace, if allowed to do so; but this can be prevented by the President, if he chooses to exercise his authority as becomes the chief Magistrate of our great and powerful country. But unfortunately Mr. Buchanan seems to regard himself as elected to submit tremblingly to any and every demand of the South, and I fear he can never rouse himself to take such action as our emergencies now require as due to the country from him. Time must show: the only thing safe to predict is, that the conduct of the South must involve her people in suffering and shame."

A few months later and the career of Captain Lyon becomes a portion of his country's history; the obscurity which has shrouded so many years of his life suddenly changes to a blaze of publicity, in the midst of which he appears as a hero. From this time there is no want of material for his biography, but rather an *embarras du richesse;* for during the last five months the journals all over the land have been full of him—his plans and movements, his victories, and his death. We shall use them freely in the rest of this sketch, trusting that the facts which it contains will excuse its lack of originality.

The prompter's bell rang on the 7th of May, 1861, and, the curtain rising, we saw Captain Lyon on the stage of action in Missouri. He was in St. Louis, in command of the Arsenal. The Police Commissioners demanded the removal of the

United States troops from all the places occupied by them outside the Arsenal grounds. Captain Lyon declined compliance with the demand, and the Commissioners referred the matter to the Governor and the Legislature. The Commissioners alleged that such occupancy was in derogation of the Constitution and the laws of the United States; and in rejoinder Captain Lyon inquired what provisions of the Constitution and laws were thus violated. The Commissioners, in support of their position, said that originally "Missouri had sovereign and exclusive jurisdiction over her whole territory," and had delegated a portion of her sovereignty to the United States over certain tracts of land for military purposes, such as arsenals, parks, &c., and the conclusion implied was, that this was the extreme limit of the right of the United States Government to occupy or touch the soil of the sovereign State of Missouri.

Whether Captain Lyon finally acceded

to the demand, may be seen by the following article from the St. Louis Republican.

St. Louis, May 10.

Unusual, and to some extent alarming, activity prevailed early yesterday morning at each rendezvous of the Home Guard and in the vicinity of the Arsenal. The men recently provided with arms from the Arsenal, to the number of several thousands, were ordered, we understand, to be at their different posts at 12 o'clock, in readiness to march as they might be commanded. A report gained some currency that General Harney was expected on the afternoon train, and that the troops were to cross the river to receive him, and escort him to the city. Very little reliance, however, was placed in this explanation of the military movements, and at about 2 o'clock P.M., the whole town became greatly agitated upon the circulation of the intelligence that some five or six thousand men were marching up Market Street, under arms, in the direction of Camp Jackson. The news proved to be correct, except as to the numbers, and in this case the report rather under-estimated the extent of the force. According to our best information, there were probably not less than seven thousand men under Captain Lyon (commanding the United States troops at this post), with about twenty pieces of artillery.

The troops, as stated before, marched at quick time up Market Street, and on arriving near Camp Jackson, rapidly surrounded it, planting batteries upon all the heights overlooking the camp. Long files of men were stationed in platoons at various points on every side, and a picket guard established covering an area of say two hundred yards. The guards, with fixed bayonets, and muskets at half cock, were instructed to allow none to pass or repass within the limits thus taken up.

By this time an immense crowd of people had assembled in the vicinity, having gone thither in carriages, buggies, rail-cars, baggage-wagons, on horseback, and on foot. Numbers of men seized rifles, shot-guns, or whatever other weapons they could lay hands upon, and rushed pell-mell to the assistance of the State troops, but were, of course, obstructed in their design. The hills, of which there are a number in the neighborhood, were literally black with people—hundreds of ladies and children stationing themselves with the throng, but, as they thought, out of harm's way.

Gen. Frost, commanding Camp Jackson, received the intelligence of the advance of the Arsenal troops with equanimity, but with some astonishment. He had heard reports that it was the design of Capt. Lyon to attack his camp, but was not at first disposed to place credence in them. So rapidly did these rumors come to him, however, that yesterday morning he addressed Capt. L. a note, of which the following is a copy:

HEAD-QUARTERS, CAMP JACKSON,
Missouri Militia, May 10, 1861.

Captain N. LYON, commanding United States Troops in and about St. Louis Arsenal.

SIR:—I am constantly in receipt of information that you contemplate an attack upon my camp, whilst I understand that you are impressed with the idea that an attack upon the Arsenal and United States troops is intended on the part of the militia of Missouri. I am greatly at a loss to know what could justify you in attacking citizens of the United States who are in the lawful performance of duties devolving upon them under the Constitution, in organizing and instructing the militia of the State in obedience to her laws, and therefore have been disposed to doubt the correctness of the information I have received. I would be glad to know from you personally whether there is any truth in the statements that are constantly poured into my ears. So far as regards any hostility being intended towards the United States, or its property or representatives, by any portion of my command, or, as far as I can learn (and I think I am fully informed), of any other part of the State forces, I can say positively that the idea has never been entertained. On the contrary, prior to your taking command of the Arsenal, I proffered to Major Bell, then in command of the very few troops constituting its guard, the service of myself and all my command, and, if necessary, the whole power of the State, to protect the United States in the full possession of all her property. Upon Gen. Harney's taking command of this department, I made the same proffer of services to him, and authorized his Adjutant-General, Capt. Williams, to communicate the fact that such had been done to the War Department. I have had no occasion since to change any of the views I entertained at that time, neither of my own volition nor through orders of my constitutional commander. I trust that after this explicit statement we may be able, by fully understanding each other, to keep far from our borders the misfortunes which so unhappily afflict our common country.

This communication will be handed to you by Col. Bowen, my Chief of Staff, who will be able to explain anything not fully set forth in the foregoing.

I am, sir, very respectfully, your obedient servant,

Brig.-Gen. D. M. FROST,
Commanding Camp Jackson, M. V. M.

Capt. L. refused to receive the above communication. He forwarded Gen. Frost the following about the time, if we are not mistaken, of the surrounding of his camp:

HEAD-QUARTERS UNITED STATES TROOPS,
St. Louis (Mo.), May 10, 1861.

Gen. D. M. FROST, Commanding Camp Jackson:

SIR: Your command is regarded as evidently hostile towards the Government of the United States.

It is, for the most part, made up of those

secessionists who have openly avowed their hostility to the General Government, and have been plotting at the seizure of its property and the overthrow of its authority. You are openly in communication with the so-called Southern Confederacy, which is now at war with the United States, and you are receiving at your camp, from the said Confederacy and under its flag, large supplies of the materiel of war, most of which is known to be the property of the United States. These extraordinary preparations plainly indicate none other but the well-known purpose of the Governor of this State, under whose orders you are acting, and whose purpose, recently communicated to the Legislature, has just been responded to by that body in the most unparalleled legislation, having in direct view hostilities to the General Government and co-operation with its enemies.

In view of these considerations, and of your failure to disperse in obedience to the proclamation of the President, and of the imminent necessities of State policy and welfare, and the obligations imposed upon me by instructions from Washington, it is my duty to demand, and I do hereby demand of you an immediate surrender of your command, with no other condition than that all persons surrendering under this demand shall be humanely and kindly treated. Believing myself prepared to enforce this demand, one half-hour's time, before doing so, will be allowed for your compliance therewith.

Very respectfully, your obedient servant,
N. Lyon,
Capt. 2d Infantry, Com. Troops.

Immediately on the receipt of the foregoing, General Frost called a hasty consultation of the officers of his staff. The conclusion arrived at was that the brigade was in no condition to make resistance to a force so numerically superior, and that only one course could be pursued—a surrender.

The demand of Capt. Lyon was accordingly agreed to. The State troops were therefore made prisoners of war, but an offer was made to release them on condition that they would take an oath to support the Constitution of the United States and would swear not to take up arms against the Government. These terms were made known to the several commands and the opportunity given to all who might feel disposed to accede to them to do so. Some eight or ten men signified their willingness; but the remainder, about eight hundred, preferred, under the circumstances, to become prisoners. (A number of the troops were absent from the camp in the city on leave.) Those who declined to take the prescribed oath, said that they had already sworn allegiance to the United States and to defend the Government, and to repeat it now would be to admit that they had been in rebellion, which they would not concede.

The preparations for the surrender and for marching, as prisoners, under the escort of the Arsenal troops, occupied an hour or two. About half-past five the prisoners left the grove and entered the road, the United States soldiers inclosing them by a single file stretched along each side of the line. A halt was ordered and the troops remained standing in the position they had deployed into on the road. The head of the column at the time rested opposite a small hill on the left as you approach the city, and the rear was on a line with the entrance to the grove. Vast crowds of people covered the surrounding grounds and every fence and housetop in the vicinity. Suddenly the sharp reports of several firearms were heard from the front of the column, and the spectators that lined the adjacent hill were seen fleeing in the greatest dismay and terror. It appeared that several members of one of the German companies, on being pressed by the crowd and receiving some blows from them, turned and discharged their pieces. Fortunately no one was injured, and the soldiers who had done the act were at once placed under arrest. Hardly, however, had tranquillity been restored, when volley after volley of rifle reports were suddenly heard from the extreme rear ranks, and men, women, and children were beheld running wildly and frantically away from the scene. Many, while running, were suddenly struck to the sod, and the wounded and dying made the late beautiful field look like a battle-ground. The wounded, who were unable to be moved, were suitably cared for on the grounds. The total number killed and injured was about twenty-five. It was reported that the Arsenal troops were attacked with stones, and a couple of shots discharged at them by the crowd before they fired. The most of the people exposed to the fire of the soldiers were citizens, with their wives and children, who were merely spectators, and took no part in any demonstration whatever. The firing was said to have been done by Boernstein's company, and at the command of an officer.

The United States troops are now in possession of Camp Jackson, with all the equipage, tents, provisions, &c. The prisoners of war are, we believe, at the Arsenal.

It is almost impossible to describe the intense exhibition of feeling which was manifested in the city. All the most frequented streets and avenues were thronged with citizens in the highest state of excitement, and loud huzzas and occasional shots were heard in various localities. Thousands upon thousands of restless human beings could be seen from almost every point on Fourth Street, all in search of the latest news. Imprecations, loud and long, were hurled into the darkening air, and the most unanimous resentment was expressed on all sides at the manner of firing into the harmless crowds near Camp Jackson. Hon. J. R. Barret, Major Uriel Wright, and other speakers addressed a large and intensely excited crowd in front of the Planters' House, and other well-known citizens were similarly engaged at various other points in the city. All the drinking saloons, restaurants, and other public resorts of similar character were closed by their proprietors, almost simultaneously, at dark; and the windows of private dwellings were fastened in fear of a general riot. Theatres and other public places of amusement were entirely out of the question, and nobody was near them. Matters of graver import were occupying the minds of the citizens, and everything but the present excitement was banished from their thoughts. Crowds of men rushed through the principal thoroughfares, bearing banners and devices suitable to their several fancies, and by turns cheering and groaning. Some were armed and others were not armed, and all seemed anxious to be at work. A charge was made on the gun store of H. E. Dimick, on Main Street, the door was broken open, and the crowd secured fifteen or twenty guns before a sufficent number of police could be collected to arrest their proceedings.

Chief McDonough marched down with about twenty policemen, armed with muskets, and succeeded in dispersing the mob and protecting the premises from further molestation. Squads of armed policemen were stationed at several of the most public corners, and the offices of the Missouri Democrat and Anzeiger des Westens were placed under guard for protection.

Four days later General Harney, who had assumed the command of the Department, issued a proclamation to the people of Michigan, in which he alluded to Captain Lyon and his capture of Camp Jackson:

"It is not proper," he said, "for me to comment upon the official conduct of my predecessor in command of this Department, but it is right and proper for the people of Missouri to know that the main avenue of Camp Jackson, recently under command of General Frost, had the name of Davis, and a principal street of the same camp that of Beauregard; and that a body of men had been received into that camp by its commander, which had been notoriously organized in the interests of the secessionists, the men openly wearing the dress and badge distinguishing the army of the so-called Southern Confederacy. It is also a notorious fact that a quantity of arms had been received into the camp, which were unlawfully taken from the United States Arsenal at Baton Rouge, and surreptitiously passed up the river in boxes marked marble.

"Upon facts like these, and having in view what occurred at Liberty, the people can draw their own inferences, and it cannot be difficult for any one to arrive at a correct conclusion as to the character and ultimate purpose of that encampment. No government in the world would be entitled to respect that would tolerate for a moment such openly treasonable preparations."

The same day the first four regiments of the United States Volunteers were formed into a brigade, as the 1st Brigade Missouri Volunteers, and Captain Lyon was elected their Brigadier-General. The next day he sent an expedition against Potosi, for the purpose of overawing the secessionists there, who were driving the Union men from their homes. It was perfectly successful, fifty or more secessionists being taken, though afterwards released on their parole of honor; a lead manufactory broken up, and one John Dean—not the Milesian gentleman of whom we have all heard, in connexion with the fair damsel Mary Ann—but the owner of the lead manufactory aforesaid, captured and held; a company of secession cavalry put to flight, and a rebel flag seized as a trophy, after which the company returned to St. Louis in triumph.

On the 21st of May the loyal portion of the community was startled with the intelligence that General Harney had entered into an arrangement with General Sterling Price, the commander of the Missouri Militia, for the purpose of maintaining the public peace. General Price pledged the whole power of the State officers to maintain order among the people of the State, and General Harney declared that this object being assured, he could have no occasion, as he had no wish, to make military movements, which might otherwise create excitement and jealousies which he most earnestly desired to avoid.

The impression prevailed that General Harney had been overreached by the Secessionists, which was the case, but no fears were entertained in regard to General Lyon, whose remarkable energy and acuteness were every day more manifest. He ordered the steamer J. C. Swan to be seized at Harlow's Landing, thirty miles below St. Louis, and brought to the St. Louis Arsenal. This was the steamer that brought the arms from Baton Rouge, which were captured by him at Camp Jackson. About 5,000 pounds of lead, *en route* for the South, were also seized at Ironton, on the Iron Mountain Railroad. Some resistance was offered by a party of citizens, and several shots were fired on both sides, but nobody was hurt.

This was on the 22d, the day after Harney and Price had made their arrangements for a peace. Nine days later the former was recalled by the authorities in Washington, and General Lyon was left in command of the Department. Having by this time had a taste of his quality, the Secessionists began to be alarmed, and not without reason, as it was clear that he was strengthening himself to meet the exigencies of his position. On the 4th of June General Price issued a proclamation to the Brigadier-Generals commanding the several military districts in Missouri, in which he expressed his desire that the people of that State should exercise the right to choose their own position in any contest which might be forced upon them, unaided by any military force whatever, and spoke of the armistice, as it were, into which he had wheedled the unsuspecting Harney.

"The Federal Government, however," he

said, "has thought proper to remove General Harney from the command of the Department of the West, but as the successor of General Harney will certainly consider himself and his Government in honor bound to carry out this agreement in good faith, I feel assured that his removal should give no cause of uneasiness to our citizens for the security of their liberties and property. I intend, on my part, to adhere both in its spirit and to the letter. The rumor in circulation, that it is the intention of the officers now in command of this Department to disarm those of our citizens who do not agree in opinion with the Administration at Washington, and put arms in the hands of those who, in some localities of this State, are supposed to sympathize with the views of the Federal Government, are, I trust, unfounded. The purpose of such a movement could not be misunderstood, and it would not only be a violation of the agreement referred to, and an equally plain violation of our constitutional right, but a gross indignity to the citizens of the State, which would be resisted to the last extremity."

This certainty that General Lyon would "carry out this agreement in good faith," was not destined to be realized, and the Secessionists began to scatter from St. Louis. A week later they sought an interview with General Lyon, Governor Jackson, General Price, and other prominent traitors coming from Jefferson City for that purpose. In the course of the interview, which lasted four hours, they demanded that no United States troops should march through, or quarter in Missouri. General Lyon refused to agree to the demand, asserting the right of the Government to send its troops wherever it pleased, and promising to protect all loyal citizens in their rights, and to fight all disloyal ones, whom he should meet in arms. Governor Jackson returned to Jefferson City, a wiser, and possibly a sadder, man. Learning that General Lyon was on the way to attack him, he evacuated that place early on the morning of the 14th. Soon after sunrise but few of the rebels were to be found in the town. Orders were given by Governor Jackson for the destruction of the Moreau bridge, four miles down the Missouri, and General Price attended to the demolition of the telegraph. All the cars and locomotives that could be used were taken by the rebels in their flight, and as fast as they crossed streams they secured themselves from pursuit by burning the bridges. They were quite cautious in concealing their place of destination from the loyal men of Jefferson, but it was evident that they were bound for Booneville, forty miles above, and one of the strongest Secession towns in the State.

General Lyon arrived at Jefferson City shortly after their departure, and was warmly welcomed by the mass of the citizens. A day or two later he planned an excursion, which is thus described in the *St. Louis Democrat.*

"Head-quarters, Department of the West,
Booneville, Mo, June 17, 1861.

"The steamers A. McDowell, Iatan, and City of Louisiana, left Jefferson City yesterday afternoon at two o'clock, and reached a point a mile below Providence last night, where it was thought best to lie up a few hours.. Three companies of Boernstein's regiment, under his command, were left to protect the capital. We were cheered enthusiastically by the little town of Marion, as we passed there yesterday evening. This morning we took an early start, and reached Rocheport before six o'clock, where we made a short stop, but found the people mostly surly and not disposed to be communicative. We learned, however, that the enemy were in considerable force a few miles below this place, and preparing to make a vigorous defence. Leaving there, and taking the steam ferry-boat Paul Wilcox with us, we ran up steadily till we had passed the foot of the island eight miles below here, and seeing a battery on the bluffs, and scouts hastening to report our arrival, we fell back to a point opposite to the foot of the island, and at seven o'clock A.M. disembarked on the south shore, where the bottom land between the river and bluffs is some mile and a half wide. No traitors were visible there, and the troops at once took the river road for this city. Following this road somewhat over a mile and a half, to where it ascends the bluffs, several shots from our scouts announced the driving in of the enemy's pickets.

"We continued to ascend a gently undulating slope for nearly half a mile, when the enemy were reported in full force near the summit of the next swell of ground, about three hundred yards from our front. The enemy were exceedingly well posted, having every advantage in the selection of their ground; but, as you will see, it has been clearly demonstrated that one secessionist is hardly superior to many more than his equal number.

"Arriving at the brow of the ascent,

Capt. Totten opened the engagement by throwing a few nine-pounder explosives into their ranks, while the infantry filed oblique right and left and commenced a terrible volley of musketry, which was for a short time well replied to, the balls flying thick and fast about our ears, and occasionally wounding a man on our side. The enemy were posted in a lane running towards the river from the road along which the grand army of the United States were advancing, and in a brick house on the north-east corner of the junction of the two roads. A couple of bombs were thrown through the east wall of that house, scattering the enemy in all directions. The well-directed fire of the German Infantry, Lieut.-Col. Schaeffer, on the right, and Gen. Lyon's company of regulars and part of Col. Blair's regiment on the left of the road, soon compelled the enemy to present an inglorious aspect. They clambered over the fence into a field of wheat, and again formed in line just on the brow of the hill.

They then advanced some twenty steps to meet us, and for a short time the cannons were worked with great rapidity and effect. Just at this time the enemy opened a galling fire from a grove just on the left of our centre, and from a shed beyond and still further to the left.

"The skirmish now assumed the magnitude of a battle. The commander, Gen. Lyon, exhibited the most remarkable coolness, and preserved throughout that undisturbed presence of mind shown by him alike in the camp, in private life, and on the field of battle. 'Forward on the extreme right;' 'Give them another shot, Captain Totten,' echoed above the roar of musketry clear and distinct, from the lips of the general, who led the advancing column. Our force was 2,000 in all, but not over 500 participated at any one time in the battle. The enemy, as we have since been reliably informed, were over 4,000 strong, and yet, twenty minutes from the time when the first gun was fired, the rebels were in full retreat, and our troops occupying the ground on which they first stood in line. The consummate cowardice displayed by the "seceshers" will be more fully understood when I add that the spurs or successive elevations now became more abrupt, steep, and rugged, the enemy being fully acquainted with their ground, and strong positions behind natural defences, orchards, and clumps of trees offering themselves every few yards. Nothing more, however, was seen of the flying fugitives until about one mile west of the house of William M. Adams, where they were first posted. Just there was Camp Vest, and a considerable force seemed prepared to defend the approaches to it. Meanwhile, a shot from the iron howitzer on the McDowell announced to us that Captain Voester, with his artillery men, and Captain Richardson's company of infantry, who were left in charge of the boats, were commencing operations on the battery over a mile below Camp West. This but increased the panic among the invincible (?) traitors, and Captain Totten had but to give them a few rounds before their heels were again in requisition, and Captains Cole and Miller, at the head of their companies, entered and took possession of the enemy's deserted breakfast tables.

"About twenty horses had by this time arrived within our lines with vacant saddles, and the corps reportorial were successively mounted on chosen steeds. The amount of plunder secured in Camp West, or Bacon, as the citizens here call it, from the name of the gentleman owning a fine house close by, was very large. One thousand two hundred shoes, twenty or thirty tents, quantities of ammunition, some fifty guns of various patterns, blankets, coats, carpet sacks, and two secession flags were included in the sum total.

"Leaving Captain Cole in command of the camp, we pushed on towards Booneville, chasing the cowardly wretches who outmanned us two to one. The McDowell now came along up in the rear and off to the right from our troops, and having a more distinct view of the enemy from the river, and observing their intention to make another stand at the Fair Grounds, one mile east of here, where the State has an armory extemporized, Captain Voester again sent them his compliments from the old howitzer's mouth, which, with a couple of shots from Captain Totten, and a volley from Lothrop's detachment of rifles, scattered the now thoroughly alarmed enemy in all directions. Their flight through the village commenced soon after 8 o'clock, and continued till after 11 o'clock. Some three hundred crossed the river, many went south, but the bulk kept on westwardly. A good many persons were taken at the different points of battle, but it is believed the enemy secured none of ours.

"Captain Richardson had landed below, and, with the support of the howitzer from the steamer McDowell, captured their battery, consisting of two 6-pounders (with which they intended to sink our fleet), twenty prisoners, one caisson, and eight horses with military saddles. The enemy did not fire a shot from their cannon. Speaking of prizes, the brilliant achievement in that line was by our reverend friend, W. A. Pill, chaplain of the First regiment. He had charge of a party of four men, two mounted and two on foot, with which to take charge of the wounded. Ascending the brow of a hill, he suddenly came upon a company of twenty-four rebels, armed with revolvers, and fully bent upon securing a place of safety for their carcasses. Their intentions, however, were considerably modified, when the parson ordered them to halt, which they did, surrendering their arms. Surrounded by the squad of five men, they were then marched on board the Louisiana, prisoners of war. The parson also captured two other secessionists during the day, and at one time, needing a wagon and horses for the wounded, and finding friendly suggestions wasted on a stubborn old rebel, placed a revolver at his head, and the desired articles were forthcoming. In time of peace the preacher had prepared for war.

"After passing the Fair Grounds, our troops came slowly towards town. They were met on the east side of the creek by Judge Miller of the District Court, and other prominent citizens, bearing a flag of truce, in order to assure our troops of friendly feelings sustained by three-fourths of the inhabitants, and if possible prevent the shedding of innocent blood. They were met cordially by General Lyon and Colonel Blair, who promised, if no resistance was made to their entrance, that no harm need be feared. Major O'Brien soon joined the party from the city, and formally surrendered it to the Federal forces. The troops then advanced, headed by the Major and General Lyon, and were met at the principal corner of the street by a party bearing and waving that beautiful emblem under which our armies gather and march forth conquering and to conquer. The flag party cheered the troops, who lustily returned the compliment. American flags are now quite thick on the street, and secessionists are nowhere.

"The enemy had two regiments of 1,800 men, under command of Colonel J. S. Marmaduke of Arrow Rock, and nine hundred cavalry, besides other companies whose muster-rolls have not been captured. Horace H. Brand was Lieutenant-Colonel of Marmaduke's regiment. It was reported, and for some time generally believed, that he was among the dead, but he has since been heard from, taking a meal several miles away. Governor Jackson was also seen at 3 o'clock this afternoon, at a blacksmith's shop, about fifteen miles from here. General Price left on Sunday morning on the steamer H. D. Bacon for Arrow Rock. His *health* was *very poor* when he left.

"One can hardly imagine the joy expressed and felt by the loyal citizens when the

Federal troops entered the city. Stores, which had been closed all day, began to open, the national flag was quickly run up on a secession pole, cheers for the Union, Lyon, Blair, and Lincoln, were frequently heard, and everything betokened the restoration of peace, law, and order. True men say that had the troops delayed ten days longer, it would have been impossible for them to remain in safety. Irresponsible vagabonds had been taking guns wherever they could find them, and notifying the most substantial and prosperous citizens to leave. As a specimen of the feeling here, Mr. McPherson, proprietor of the City Hotel, denounces the whole secession movement as the greatest crime committed since the crucifixion of our Saviour.

"At one time, when bullets were flying thick and General Lyon was at the head of the column, mounted, he undertook to dismount, that his position might be a trifle less conspicuous, when his horse suddenly jumped with fright, throwing the general to the ground, but without injuring him seriously. The rumor suddenly spread through the ranks that General Lyon had been shot from his horse, and the indignation and cries of vengeance were terrific. At the Fair Grounds several hundred muskets were seized at the armory, where flint locks were being altered. Captain Totten says he fired about 100 rounds of ball, shell, and canister.

"The following interesting documents were found among others equally interesting and more decidedly treasonable:

"HEAD-QUARTERS FIRST REG'T RIFLES, M. S. G.,
Booneville, Mo., June 14, 1861.

"GENERAL ORDERS, No. 3.—The commanders of companies of the regiment and of the troops attached will bring their companies to Booneville with the greatest despatch. They will proceed to move the instant this order is received, bringing with them all arms and ammunition it is possible to procure. The expenses of said movements will be paid by the State. All orders of a prior date conflicting with this from any head-quarters whatever will be disobeyed. By order of

"Colonel J. S. Marmaduke.
"John W. Wood, Adjutant."

"Captain—Hurry on day and night. Everybody, citizens and soldiers, must come, bringing their arms and ammunition. Time is everything. In great haste,

" J. S. Marmaduke."

The day after the battle General Lyon released his prisoners, most of whom were young men, in consideration of their youth, and of the deceit that had been practised upon them, requiring their pledge not again to bear arms against the United States.

On the morning of the 3rd of July he left with upwards of two thousand men for the Southwest, whither the Secessionists were swarming, under Price and the ubiquitous Ben McCullough. His force increased as he advanced, until it amounted to ten thousand men. He had about that number on the 20th at Springfield, but from that time it decreased, the term for which many of the volunteers had enlisted having expired. On the 1st of August it had dwindled down to six thousand.

A report which reached him at this time gave rise to the belief that General McCullough designed to attack him at Springfield, by two columns moving from Cassville and Sarcoxie. The federal scouts reported their force at about fifteen thousand in each division, and they were reported within twenty miles of the town and advancing from Cassville. General Lyon ordered his entire command, with the exception of a small guard, to rendezvous at Crane Creek, ten miles south of Springfield.

"The march," says one who participated in it (the Western War Correspondent of *The World*) "commenced at 5 o'clock on the afternoon of the 1st. The baggage wagons, one hundred and eighty in number, were scattered over a distance of three miles. The camp at Crane Creek was reached about 10 o'clock, the men marching slowly and making frequent halts to get the benefit of shade or water.

"Early next morning, after making a hasty meal, the line of march was resumed. We were joined by the division from Camp McClellan, and, with cavalry and skirmishers ahead, pushed on as fast as the nature of the country would admit. This day, like its predecessor, was intensely hot. The extreme temperature, and the fine dust which enveloped the train in clouds, produced intolerable thirst. The country is of the hilly kind which just falls below the standard of mountainous. After leaving Springfield, which is said to be the summit of the Bark Mountains, we pass along the ridge which divides the waters which fall into the Missouri and White rivers. Streams there were none to mention; though traceable on the map, they are at this season only distinguishable by their dry rocky beds.

Water was hardly to be had, the few springs and wells in the neighborhood being either emptied by drouth or by the men. The ridges and sides of the limestone hills were covered for the most part with stunted oak saplings, which rarely afforded shade for horse and rider. The midsummer sun travelled through an unclouded sky like a ball of fire, scorching all animated nature in his way. The men, however, kept up their spirits tolerably well, and as at every few miles loyal citizens were met, informing us that the enemy was but a few miles ahead, every prospect for a grand fight was the common opinion.

"At about 11 o'clock, as the advanced guard was rising the crest of a hill, sixteen miles from here, the skirmishers discovered several mounted men in the road. Word was passed back, when Captain Totten ordered a six-pounder to the front, and just as the men were in the act of leaving the house of one of their secession friends he sent a shell by the gunpowder line, which burst over the house. When this unexpected messenger dropped in among them they scampered away down the hill, so that when we arrived at the top nothing was to be seen but a moving cloud of dust. A light wagon, loaded with cooked provisions, was discovered on the road, which was shared by our famished men and eaten with infinite gusto. Bedding and other accoutrements were found around the buildings, indicating a lengthened sojourn.

"Our painful march was then continued with more caution, the woods and thickets being examined on either side of the road for ambuscades and surprises. Arrived at Dug Springs, some three miles further, we could perceive as we entered the valley by one hill dense columns of dust moving in various directions along the base and sides of the hills at the opposite end. The advance continued, the column drawn up ready for action. By the aid of glasses, bodies of men, both mounted and on foot, could be seen, and presently we could hear the sharp crack of the rifles of our advanced guard. The flags were displayed, and all the indications seemed to point to a great battle, the position of the enemy being a strong one, and his force evidently numerous.

"As there was no advance from the valorous rebels, spite of our coaxing, the day far spent, and the prospect for camping ground ahead not very brilliant, a retrograde movement was ordered, with a view of coaxing the enemy from his position.

"In order to understand the position of the parties, imagine an oblong basin of five miles in length, surrounded by hills from which spurs projected into the main hollow, covered with occasional thickets and oak openings. The winding of the road round the spurs had the effect of concealing the strength of each party from the other, so that from the top of each successive ridge could be seen the rear of the enemy's forces. At about five o'clock a brisk interchange of shots was commenced by our skirmishers, Captain Steele's regular infantry taking the lead on the left, supported by a company of cavalry, the rest of the column being back some distance. Presently we could see a column of infantry approaching from the woods with the design of cutting off our infantry. Capt. Stanley immediately drew up his men, and, as soon as within range, they opened fire from their Sharp's carbines, when several volleys were exchanged. The number of the enemy's infantry was seemingly about five hundred; our cavalry not quite a hundred and fifty. The infantry kept up the firing for some minutes, when some enthusiastic lieutenant giving the order to "charge," some twenty-five of the gallant regulars rushed forward upon the enemy's lines, and, dashing aside the threatening bayonets of the sturdy rebels, hewed down the ranks with fearful slaughter. Capt. Stanley, who was amazed at the temerity of the little band, was obliged to sustain the order, but before he could reach his little company, they had broken the ranks of the cowards, who outnumbered them as twenty to one. Some of the rebels who were wounded asked, in utter astonishment, 'Whether these were men or devils—they fight so?'

"The ground was left in our possession, being strewn with muskets, shot-guns, pistols, etc. Our men seized some fifteen muskets and the same number of horses and mules, and rode off, when a large force of the enemy's cavalry was seen approaching from the woods, numbering some three hundred or more. At the instant when they had formed in an angle, Capt. Totten, who had planted a six and a twelve-pounder upon the overlooking hill, sent a shell right over them; in another minute the second —a twelve-pound shell, a very marvel of gunnery practice—which landed right at their feet, exploding, and scattering the whole body in the most admired disorder. The third, fourth, fifth, and sixth were sent into their midst. The horsemen could not control their horses, and in a minute not an enemy was to be seen anywhere. Captain Granger, of the artillery, was so pleased with the execution that he rode out to the spot, where he discovered several pools of blood on the ground, as if the shell had done great damage, one double-barrelled shot-gun being bent by the fragments of the shell.

"The praise of all tongues was upon the magnificent charge of our cavalry. The men, actuated by a supreme disdain for the novices who had but recently left the plough for the musket, determined to give them a real taste of war at the onset; and they must have given the poor deluded fools a bitter foretaste, with their navy revolvers and carbines. Two of the lieutenants returned with their swords stained, with the blood of men they had run through and through, up to the hilt. One horse which was led home, was pierced by nine balls; another with sides so covered with gore as to conceal the wounds. Four of their wounded men were afterwards picked up on the ground, some of them fatally. Unfortunately our loss, as might be expected, was severe. Four of our gallant regulars were brought in dead, and five wounded, one of which has since died. The loss of the enemy cannot be far from forty, and their wounded fully a hundred. Secession accounts admit their loss was heavy.

"Although the entire action cannot be raised to the dignity of a great battle, for the whole affair lasted less than half an hour, it was in reality a great triumph. Our advanced cavalry was alone engaged on our part, and they successfully fought and drove off a force ten times their number. It moreover revealed the fighting animus of the enemy; it revealed the state of their armament, and afforded a brilliant example for our expectant troops.

"All supposed, when the crack of the cannon and whistling of shell were heard in such quick succession, that the battle was begun, and that a trial at arms was to ensue ere nightfall. Our men were under arms, cannon in position, until the news of the inglorious retreat of the vaunting rebels dispelled the prospect. The camps were then pitched and the necessary precautions taken against attack. No description can do justice to the labors of the day. When the morning dawned the men were put in motion. The heat was insufferable, the incessant running about among the brush for miles on both sides of the main road created the most suffocating thirst. The tongue became swollen, the sweat was blinding, and the dust profuse. Even the hardiest of men were glad to find shelter for a moment in the shade of some canebrake. The few wells or springs in the vicinity had given out. Water was not to be had; towards evening two dollars and a half being offered for a canteen of warm ditch water. Many were victims of sunstroke and exhaustion, and never were a set of men more grateful than when the burning sun cast his declining shadow over the western hills. The night was broken occasionally by the report of musket shots from our sentinels. Two or three stragglers were brought in as prisoners, who stated that they belonged to the command of General Rains, and seemed glad enough to be captured. They reported that the army of McCullough was five miles in the rear, and that accessions were being recruited from all the adjoining counties. This information agreed with that gained from the prisoners, and betrayed the weakness of the enemy; said they, 'we have had nothing but fresh beef and unbolted flour to eat for many days.' They were forced northward by starvation, and the Union men must either flee or be taken prisoners, while the state rights gentry must join their force or be plundered; they would find, however, that plunder attended either alternative. In this way they had recruited thousands, leaving a desert behind them more complete than the locusts. Forage, wheat, eatables and drinkables, in any quantity, did not escape them. Clothing and trinkets of little or no value, all seized. They are the most complete land pirates this continent ever saw.

"*August* 2.—We resumed the line of march at sunrise; the ground of yesterday's operations was carefully gone over in search of the much dreaded 'masked batteries.' Gaining the summit of the hill from which the rebels had sallied on the day previous, we found a sad spectacle. A house by the wayside, with four wounded men in the first room, in the second one severely wounded in the back and shoulder, in the third a corpse stretched out with the face quite black. At the well, close by the house, the pools in the little stream were red as blood for thirty yards, where they had washed their wounded. The men stated they had only been picked off the field that morning, and that there were many more who had been carried off with the retreating army. They confirmed substantially the reports of the captives.

"Descending into the next valley, we could just perceive, by the dense clouds of dust, that the enemy were but a few miles ahead. Two guns were placed upon an eminence; upon seeing a column of troops moving up a ravine, and when at the distance of three-quarters of a mile, we opened fire upon them, when they rapidly retreated. We afterwards learned that this was a scouting party, who had crossed over from Marionsville, after taking what provisions and men they could press into their service by their very summary process. The shell struck the chimney of a house in which the officers were dining. They did not wait for the dessert to be served.

"Arriving at Curran, twenty-six miles from Springfield, we encamped, to take advantage of the good water. Our position was much exposed, but from the exhibitions of valor for the past few days we stood in little fear of an attack. Five prisoners were brought in by our skirmishers, one of which, upon being questioned by General Lyon, manifested considerable impertinence; his actions being suspicious he was carefully watched, and when told to rise from the ground a revolver was found under him. A deserter came in from the other camp, who stated that he was impressed into their service in Missouri; their camp was six miles to the north, and strongly intrenched; had eight pieces of cannon, and, though his comrades said they had fifteen thousand men, his opinion was about six or seven thousand. Quite a little excitement was created throughout the camp in the morning by a report that we were surrounded, which was caused by the appearance of troops on our rear—doubtless a portion of the roving bands desirous of rejoining their command. A squad of about forty entered our column and chatted with our men under the impression that they were in the army of Rains, until they saw our artillery coming up, when they inquired 'Whose troops we were?' Upon being informed 'General Lyon's' they made a hasty exit into the dense woods, one of the staff officers ordering the men to fire upon them, but they had made good their escape.

"Our troops had mistaken them also for the 'Home Guards,' which are accustomed to act as guides and scouts, and thus they missed, by a narrow chance, the opportunity of bagging the whole of them, and their horses and muskets.

"The names of our killed are Corporal Klein, privates Givens and Devlin.

"Springfield, August 6th.

"After another day's hardship and night's repose, the morning dawned upon us with its fierce glare. General Lyon finding himself short of provisions, his men weary and footsore, many of them sick from intemperate use of water and green fruits, with a powerful enemy encamped in front, whom he could not chase by reason of the precautions against surprises and flank movements—moreover, a large force of the enemy in the direction of Sarcoxie, and the necessity of keeping open his communication with Springfield—called a consultation with Brigadier-Generals Sweeny, Siegel; Majors Schofield, Shepherd, Conant, Sturgis; Captains Totten and Shaeffer, when it was determined to retire towards Springfield. This conclusion seems to be well founded, when we reflect that the provisions for such an army must be transported from Rolla at a great risk of capture. Nothing could be found either for man or horse on the track of the rebels.

"Hardly had the decision been declared, when one of the cavalry scouts announced that he had witnessed the departure of McCullough's camp in the direction of Sarcoxie, describing the train as long as that usually pertaining to an army of seven thousand men.

"On Sunday morning we retraced our steps, leaving Curran, Stone co., the furthest point of our expedition, with reluctance at not meeting the object of our search, but with hearts gladdened that we were once more to be placed beyond the danger of starvation. We marched thirteen miles during the day in a broiling sun. Several of our men fell from the fatigue and heat; two reported died from sun-stroke.

"At Cane Creek we found another deserter who had been forced into a Louisiana regiment, and had accepted the first chance to escape. He is a German, and has a brother in the Missouri Volunteers. His statements confirm those of the other deserter. His regiment left New Orleans one thousand and fifty strong, and when he left it, death, disease, and desertion had reduced it to seven hundred. His regiment was well drilled and armed. Three Arkansas regiments were armed with old smooth-bore muskets; the balance with odds and ends of all kinds, some few being without arms. Two Texan regiments are daily expected, with two brass guns. He gives a deplorable account of their commissariat and subsistence departments. He is kept in close custody, both for his own protection, and as a precaution against fraud.

"We reached Springfield to-day, and were much surprised to learn that the inhabitants had been the victims of the most unreasonable fright—a report having been spread during the night that the enemy was about to attack the town. Singularly enough nearly all the pickets came into town, instead of remaining at their posts. I ought in justice to say that these were 'Home Guards,' who have been mustered into the service to meet the emergency.

"We brought in sixteen prisoners, most of them taken in a hostile attitude towards the government. We witnessed a very salutary way of treating rebels. Two or three prominent secessionists, who at one time were accounted respectable, are busily hauling the debris from the streets, and performing other such municipal duties under guard, greatly to the edification of a crowd of boys and negroes. We think this is the happy medium between hanging our prisoners and swearing them."

The position of General Lyon was a critical one, in spite of the victory he had won, he was so largely out-numbered by the enemy. Why he was not reinforced by General Fremont, who was in charge of the Department, has not yet been explained. Perhaps he shared the delusion under which most of us labored prior to Bull's Run—the childish folly of underrating our enemy. Not so General Lyon, for knowing the strait in which he stood, he telegraphed from Springfield to Washington to General Fremont, before the latter had left New York for St. Louis, imploring succor. And after he had reached St. Louis, he sent three or four special messengers thither for the same purpose, but they failed. One of these agents was a former Secretary of State, another a member of Congress, both from the south-western part of the State, where the danger lay. Governor Gamble, too, added his own urgent advice that General Lyon be reinforced; but to no purpose. Nor were reinforcements all that he stood in need of, for at this very time his command had but half rations of bread, and for the next ten days, until the next battle, in fact when he was killed, and they were overpowered, but half rations of bread and water!

So, at least, it is charged, and apparently with truth. There may be some mistake in the matter (we trust there is), but there can be no mistake in the fact that General Fremont has not done what was expected of him in Missouri. Did we expect too much, remembering what General Lyon had done? Under his energetic management the State was nearly cleared of rebels, and the Union cause was triumphing. Now —but we have no heart to go on, remembering the fall of Lexington. We are not unfriendly to General Fremont in this, but we are more friendly to our country, for whom, as it now seems to us, a brave life has been needlessly sacrificed. *Fiat Justitia, ruat cœlum.*

A glimpse of General Lyon, or rather of

his body-guard at this time may not be uninteresting. It was composed of ten athletic St. Louis butchers, each mounted on a powerful horse and armed with a heavy cavalry sword and a pair of navy revolvers; each wore a light hat turned up on the left side, and decorated with a white ostrich plume. Accompanied by half a dozen of these savage looking fellows, he might often be seen spurring along the line; or they might be seen in small squads, or singly, galloping fiercely to the front or the rear, or straight out into the open country. If he went into a house, a half dozen of them stood in front like iron statues at the bridle of their horses. If he scoured along in advance of the train, the clanking of their long sabres was heard beside him. Stop where he would, there was a stolid squad of white-plumed horsemen awaiting patiently his movements. They were fearless riders—jumping fences on a dead run, leaping ditches, galloping down steep descents, and, in fact, never riding less fast than their horses could run, unless compelled by some urgent necessity. Independent of their duty as body-guards, they acted as messengers, scouts, &c. They were commanded by a lieutenant, and were noted from their appearance and daring horsemanship.

On the 10th of August, three months after the capture of Camp Jackson, General Lyon was no more. He fell at the battle of Wilson's Creek, which is thus described by the Special Correspondent of *The New York Herald:*

"SPRINGFIELD, Mo., Aug. 10, 1861.

"After the occurrences of the 3d and 4th inst., and the falling back of the Union troops upon Springfield, the rebels made an advance, and on the evening of the 6th formed their camp upon Wilson's Creek, about ten miles from Springfield, on the Fayetteville road. Reports of spies, deserters, and a few prisoners, made it certain that they were in force from eight to twenty thousand, and were provided with from eight to sixteen pieces of brass cannon. On the evening of the 7th, General Lyon formed a plan of night surprise, but the project was abandoned, and nothing of importance occurred until the evening of the 9th. On that evening the plan was formed of attacking them simultaneously at either end of the camp, which extended for some three miles along the banks of the creek.

DISPOSITION OF THE UNION FORCES.

" General Siegel was sent to the extreme left, to begin the attack on that side, having with him a force of twelve hundred men, and six pieces of light artillery under command of Major Schaeffer. General Lyon led the main column, which was to open battle on the right, consisting of three companies First infantry, Captain Plummer; two companies Second infantry, Captain Steele; one company Fourth artillery, recruits, Lieutenant Lothrop; Captains Totten's and Dubois' batteries, six pieces each; Missouri First regiment, Colonel Andrews; Kansas First, Colonel Deitzler; Kansas Second, Colonel Mitchell; Iowa First, Colonel Bates, and one battalion from Second Missouri, under Major Osterhaus. In addition were several companies of Home Guards, a part of whom did good service, but the majority proved an intolerable nuisance, running like frightened deer at the least alarm, and getting in the way of others.

MOVING TO THE ATTACK.

"The whole force left Springfield about sunset on the 9th, the left column taking the Fayetteville road, and the right the road leading to Mount Vernon, leaving them at proper points for making detours to enclose the rebel camp. Your correspondent joined the right column, under General Lyon, as that promised to be most actively engaged. Midnight found us in a hay field, four miles from the rebel position, and as it was not deemed prudent to approach nearer before morning, the men were permitted to get what sleep they could extract from the hard ground during the few hours preceding dawn.

"At a few minutes before four, the whole column was again in motion. It was not long before the camp appeared in sight, located, as we anticipated, along Wilson's Creek. On either side of the stream, the valley, averaging some twenty rods in width, was bounded by a range of low and gently sloping hills, covered with a scanty, but occasionally dense growth of scrub oaks, of a few feet in height. Portions of these slopes, together with parts of the valley, had been cleared and turned into corn and wheat fields; the latter had just been visited by the sickle, but the former was still in luxuriant growth, affording complete concealment to either foot or horsemen. The rebels had selected those points which admitted of the best defence as positions for their men and batteries, these being mrinly on the north side of the creek. The low oaks, with which the entire camp was surrounded, prevented our seeing many movements until almost at the last moment, and the same cause did much to hinder the aim of both artillery and riflemen. At ten minutes past five the rebel pickets were seen and driven in, and we rapidly moved forward to take position opposite the rebel battery. This we secured on a gently sloping hill, which had been the extreme of the rebel camp, as several wagons, a few tents, numerous cooking utensils, and other et ceteras of a soldier's life, plainly indicated.

THE BATTLE.

"At a distance of eight hundred yards from the rebel battery, Captain Totten unlimbered his guns and was speedily joined by Captain Dubois. Captain Totten opened the battle with a twelve-pound shell, and was promptly answered by the rebels. In a few minutes all our pieces were engaged with an equal number of the enemy's cannon, both sides firing with great rapidity. The First Missouri regiment was placed in position to support the battery, with Major Osterhaus's battalion on the extreme right to act as skirmishers. To the left of our line was a ravine, with precipitous sides; adjoining this ravine was a cornfield, and beyond the latter was a wheat stubblefield. Captains Plummer and Gilbert, with three companies of regulars, and Captain Wright, with two companies of Home Guards, were sent to occupy these fields, and prevent the enemy from making a flank movement upon the battery. The rebels did not long allow our forces to wait in line with their rifles unused, but commenced a fire of musketry upon Osterhaus's battalion and those of the First Missouri on the right. After two or three rounds of Minie balls, the firing became general along the line of this regiment, and an attempt at a charge was broken up and the enemy forced to retire. At about the time of the commencement of the firing by the First Missouri those on our left found themselves busily engaged in the cornfield with a large body of rebel troops that had been sent out to oppose them. The Home Guards, as usual, fell back to a safer locality, and the regulars, finding skirmishing in the corn more destructive to themselves than to their opponents, from the latter knowing well the ground, fell back to the edge of the field and succeeded in there holding position. The fire against the regulars before they fell back was particularly heavy and well directed, as the corn afforded a fine screen behind which to take near and deliberate aim. The regulars gave return shots whenever they obtained sight of an enemy, and are confident that they did much towards thinning the rebel ranks.

"The First Missouri troop, who were acting as a support to the battery in front, stood their ground like veterans, and sent many a Minie ball true to its aim. As much of the firing against them was from weapons inferior to theirs, they had the enemy at a slight advantage when placed man to man, and though finally much cut up and forced to retire, they were not withdrawn till they had three successive times repulsed the rebels. On each of these occasions the enemy brought fresh troops into the field, and it is believed that during the entire day they did not bring the same force twice into action except in one or two flank movements. When the Missouri First was withdrawn, after they had been under fire an hour and a half, the Kansas First and Second, with the Iowa First, were placed in the front, the latter being to the right of the Kansas troops and further towards the rear, thus keeping the Iowa partly in reserve. The rebels again came up in stronger force than ever, but were twice driven back by the Kansans—the latter, in both instances, bringing their bayonets to the charge and pursuing for some distance down the slope. They would have followed up to the battery had not their officers feared that the retreat might be a *ruse* to draw them into an ambuscade, the scanty growth of trees and bushes being admirably adapted for forming an ambush. All this time Lieutenant Lothrop's regulars were lying down to the right of Dubois's battery, waiting for a proper opportunity to come into action. The lieutenant himself sat on his horse in front of his men, displaying the most imperturbable coolness. 'Don't dodge,' said he to a reporter, who shall be nameless, as that individual turned his head aside to allow a ball to pass; 'don't dodge, for you might put your head exactly where a ball was coming, and then we should be minus a reporter.' About the time the Kansas took the place of the First Missouri, Lieutenant Lothrop's men were ordered in front of the battery to clear the brush of some rebel skirmishers known to be lying there. As they advanced and extended their line to the ravine on the left, a brisk fire was opened upon them, both from the bushes in front and the bank of the ravine on their left flank, but they succeeded in dislodging the enemy. It was then discovered that the rebel skirmishing in front was partly to draw attention from a large body of rebel infantry that was advancing about six hundred yards from our left, with the evident intention of outflanking us and falling on our rear. There appeared to be one full regiment, some six or eight companies, and about fifteen hundred men not in ranks. Captain Dubois brought his battery to bear upon them, and sent shell, grape, and canister directly in their midst, causing a hasty and confused retreat. A large body of them made a rush for an opening in the fence, behind which was a clump of timber, and, as they were crowding through, two twelve-pounder spherical case-shot were exploded among them, leaving the dead and wounded thick upon the ground. Our rear was not for some time again menaced in that direction.

"Very soon after this it was seen that the rebel cavalry, about eight hundred strong, was forming in the rear of our right to make a charge upon the ambulances, which were being brought up for the use of the wounded. Captain Wood's Kansas Rangers and two companies of Second Kansas Infantry, which happened near the rear at this time, drew up to resist them. As the cavalry came on the infantry opened with a volley, but did not succeed in checking their advance. When they were within less than two hundred yards of our lines, Captain Totten opened upon them with two rounds from his entire battery, which had been hastily brought into position unknown to the rebels. The fire was diagonally across the body, and each shot cut its lane entirely through, leaving dead and wounded horses and riders mingled indiscriminately together. The charge was broken, and the rebel cavalry made a disorderly retreat to the timber. Some twenty horses were galloping riderless about the field, and were secured by our men. The fight was again renewed with vigor in the front, and the

Iowans were brought into the thick of the contest, giving the Kansans a brief respite. They repelled an advance of rebel infantry, which no sooner disappeared than it was succeeded by a fresh force larger than the previous one. The Kansas First was again brought forward and led to the charge by General Sweeny, Colonel Deitzler having been wounded and taken to the rear.

DEATH OF GENERAL LYON.

"General Lyon was standing by his horse near the Iowans, and several among the latter asked for some one to lead them. Instantly General Lyon took command of the regiment to lead it forward, but before they reached the enemy's lines he was struck in the breast by a rifle ball and fell dead from his horse. The rebels, on seeing the approach of the Union troops, scattered and fled before the latter got sufficiently near to use the bayonet. All this transpired in a very few moments, and it was known to but few that General Lyon had fallen. The announcement of his death was not made to the soldiers till after the battle was over.

"After this but little was done on either side for upwards of half an hour, the rebels changing the position of their battery to higher ground in the rear of its former location, and Captain Totten advancing his a few rods, while Captain Dubois remained at his old post. Captain Granger, of the regular service, detected a flank movement in preparation against our left, and took three companies of the Iowa regiment to the edge of the ravine and caused them to lie down in the grass and await the enemy's approach. Very soon the column approached, Captain Dubois pouring in grape and canister when they got quite near. As soon as they had come up within short range of Captain Granger, the Iowans, taking sight without rising from their position, poured in a most destructive fire of Minie balls with terrific effect. The cannonade and musket fire were too much for the rebels, and they made the best possible use of their pedals back to a place of safety.

THE REBEL WAGON TRAIN ON FIRE.

"Immediately after this retreat flames burst forth from the rebel baggage train, which was stationed about a mile down the creek, and from the extent of the fire and the vast columns of smoke, it is supposed that the entire wagon train of the rebel army was destroyed. How the fire originated is not known, but it is supposed that the rebels, fearing a defeat and route, themselves set fire to the wagons rather than have them fall into the hands of the Unionists. They were seen to destroy some twenty wagons near their battery a short time after the fire burst forth in the large train, and it is but reasonable to suppose that the latter was turned to ashes and smoke by the owners themselves. While the conflagration was at its height the rebels made a furious attack on the Union front and right at the same time. The battery in front opened furiously, and several pieces, which had been brought against our right, under cover of the timber, played vigorously from a cleared space some eight hundred yards distant. A very large force of infantry came out in line of battle order from the very place where we had for some time expected Colonel Siegel to appear. No bayonet charges were made by either side, but the roll of musketry and the boom of cannon were more fierce and continuous than at any previous time during the day. For half an hour it was one deep, deafening roar, resounding through the air, and the field became canopied with dense clouds of smoke; the position of cannon could only be made out by the dull, red flash seen through the fog-like atmosphere, and all around was falling a pitiless shower of lead and iron. Too rapid in succession to think of counting came the smooth whistle of the common rifle ball, the shrill buzz of the Minie, the dull hum of the round ball, and above them all the sounds produced by the various descriptions of common munition. For half an hour it continued, and was ended by the repulse of the rebels, who returned no more to the field. In this last scene of the battle all the Union force on the field was in action, and one-half our loss of the day occurred at this time.

OPERATIONS OF GENERAL SIEGEL'S COMMAND.

"'Where is Siegel?' had been passing from lip to lip for an hour before this attack, and he had been anxiously looked for at the very point where the rebel infantry, bearing the secession flag, had made their appearance. As we had not heard from him since the night previous, save by the reports of his cannon, we were uncertain as to his fate, and fearful that we might fire upon him should he approach, as we did not know from what quarter to expect him. Our cannon ammunition was nearly exhausted, and several companies of infantry had expended their last round of cartridges. Major Sturgis (who took command after General Lyon's death) ordered a retreat, and the whole army took up its line of march for Springfield. Ambulances were sent back with a flag of truce to gather up the dead and wounded. The flag was received by General McCullough and Colonel McIntosh, and by nine P.M. the ambulances returned, bringing all that could be found. The battle commenced a few minutes past six A.M. and the retreat was ordered at eleven. With but a few intervals the batteries on both sides were in constant action throughout the whole, and there were few minutes when the roll of musketry could not be heard.

"To understand Colonel Siegel's position it will be necessary to explain more fully the situation of the rebel camp. Wilson's Creek has a general southerly direction; but at a farm called McNary's it makes a sharp bend to the east, follows an easterly course for two and a half miles, and then bends suddenly to the south. The Fayetteville road crosses the creek about a mile and three fourths below the upper bend. The rebel camp extended three miles along the creek—two and a half in an easterly direction, and a quarter of a mile above the upper bends towards the north, and the same distance below the lower bend towards the south. General Lyon's attack was made on the western side, just above the upper bend. Colonel Siegel marched from Springfield down (going south) the Fayetteville road, left that road four miles this side of Wilson's Creek, and turned to his left, went around the rebel camp, came into the same road two miles beyond Wilson's Creek, and marched up the Fayetteville road towards the enemy's camp. Some who saw his command coming, about daylight, from the direction of Arkansas, walked out to meet him, not dreaming of the approach of the Union forces on that side. These he allowed to get within his lines, and made prisoners of them before they discovered their mistake.

He fell upon their camp at the road, routed them and took possession, planting his cannon in the camp and playing upon them from that position. He found and took possession of the private papers of General McCullough, and one of his lieutenants was fortunate enough to secure a bag of gold. Colonel Siegel was so severely pressed that he had to abandon the camp and take position on a hill, where he served his artillery with great effect, and brought his infantry into active use. A concentrated fire was made upon his battery, killing many of his artillerymen and nearly all his horses. A dash of infantry and cavalry was then made, and five of his six cannon fell into possession of the rebels. The infantry and cavalry came so hard upon him as to compel him to retreat, which he did, bringing away nearly two hundred prisoners. His command was badly cut up and he found it impossible to make a junction with the main column. The last assault upon the main column was made just after the retreat of Colonel Siegel, and the cannon which played upon us on the right were the five that were captured. At one time, had a vigorous movement been made on our part, the rebel battery might have been taken.

"For two or three days before the battle General Lyon changed much in appearance. Since it became apparent to him that he must abandon the Southwest or have his army cut to pieces, he had lost much of his former energy and decision. To one of his staff he remarked, the evening before the battle, 'I am a man believing in presentiments, and ever since this night surprise was planned I have had a feeling I cannot get rid of that it would result disastrously. Through the refusal of government properly to reinforce me I am obliged to abandon the country. If I leave it without engaging the enemy the public will call me a coward. If I engage him I may be defeated and my command cut to pieces. I am too weak to hold

Springfield, and yet the people will demand that I bring about a battle with the very enemy I cannot keep a town against. How can this result otherwise than against us?'

"On the way to the field I frequently rode near him. He seemed like one bewildered, and often when addressed failed to give any recognition, and seemed totally unaware that he was spoken to. On the battlefield he gave his orders promptly, and seemed solicitous for the welfare of his men, but utterly regardless of his own safety. While he was standing where bullets flew thickest, just after his favorite horse was shot from under him, some of his officers interposed and begged that he would retire from the spot and seek one less exposed. Scarcely raising his eyes from the enemy he said—

"'It is well enough that I stand here. I am satisfied.'

"While the line was forming for the charge against the rebels in which he lost his life, General Lyon turned to Major Sturgis, who stood near him, and remarked—

"'I fear that the day is lost; if Colonel Siegel had been successful he would have joined us before this. I think I will lead this charge.'

"He had been wounded in the leg in an early part of the engagement—a flesh wound merely—from which the blood flowed profusely. Major Sturgis during the conversation noticed blood on General Lyon's hat, and at first supposed he had been touching it with his hand, which was wet with blood from his leg. A moment after, perceiving that it was fresh, he removed the General's hat and asked the cause of its appearance. 'It is nothing, Major, nothing but a wound in the head,' said General Lyon, turning away and mounting his horse. Without taking the hat held out to him by Major Sturgis, he addressed the Iowans he was to command with—

"'*Forward, men! I will lead you!*'

"Two minutes afterwards he lay dead on the field, killed by a rifle ball through his breast, just above the heart. In death his features wore the same troubled and puzzled expression that had been fixed upon them for the past week. His body was brought to town in the afternoon, and will be forwarded to his friends in Connecticut for interment.

"The appearance of the field throughout the day was exceedingly gloomy. The morning was cloudy, and once in the afternoon rain fell. Towards noon the sun shone out, but not clearly. The smoke from the cannon and small arms, with that from the burning train, hung over the field, seeming like a pall spread to cover the unfortunate dead. The horrors of Manassas were renewed on this battlefield. Our wounded men were bayoneted or struck over the head with musket butts. An officer, a lieutenant in the First Missouri, was taken prisoner, struck four times with a musket, and left for dead. He revived and escaped. A surgeon, who went on the field after the battle, was several times shot at and forced to retire. Later in the afternoon a flag of truce was sent to the rebel commanders, and was received.

"Union flags were several times waved to induce our men to go forward. None were taken by this *ruse*.

"At the time the enemy were advancing to outflank our left, and were repulsed by our cannonading, a rebel flag was borne prominently in their front. The man carrying it was struck by a shell, which exploded at the same moment. Another snatched up the banner, and was hurrying forward when he was killed by a canister shot. The flag was not again seen.

"Most of the shot from the rebel cannon passed over our heads. A few horses were killed by round shot, and two or three men were badly wounded with pieces of shell. With these exceptions I do not know of their artillery doing damage. Your correspondent was standing beside his horse under a tree in the rear of Capt. Totten's battery, when a six-pound shot passed through the tree top not four feet above his head. Thinking there might be a better place for observation, I changed my position some twenty rods, and I was speedily admonished of my insecurity by another ball ploughing up the ground not six feet away, and literally covering me with dirt. Upon the theory that 'lightning does not strike twice in the same place,' I kept still, and was not troubled by any more of the same sort so near me. A six-pound shot produces a sound anything but melodious. About the time the action commenced I rode past the First Missouri regiment. One of the soldiers, seeing my citizen's dress, cocked his gun and brought it to bear upon me. I ventured to ask—

"'What are you going to shoot me for?'

"'I don't know you,' was the reply, with the gun still in position.

"Just then one of the soldiers asked

where I had been since I was with them at Booneville, and my about-to-shoot friend lowered his rifle and disappeared.

"Whether the result is a victory, a defeat, or a drawn battle, I leave for the reader to decide. Our forces took a position and held it five hours. When they retired the enemy had been several times repulsed, and in the last attack driven from the field. They had burned their baggage train to prevent our getting it, and when we left the field did not attempt to pursue us. Upwards of an hour after our departure they returned and took possession, rendering it necessary that our ambulances should go out under a flag of truce. The rebel troops outnumbered the Unionists at least four to one, and some of our officers estimate their strength as fully six times that of ours."

POLITICAL WRITINGS.

I.

OUR CAUSE—OUR CANDIDATE.

Our cause is to honor labor and elevate the laborer; our candidate, Abe Lincoln.

Our cause we know to be the noblest of human aspirations; our candidate we believe fit, both in motive and capacity, for the attainment of this cause.

Labor is the only source of wealth, and through the application of its productive means is power alone obtained; and to control these means, the product of labor, to the attainment of power, do princes exhaust their policies of state, priests their subtleties of theology, and demagogues and designing men every artifice of hypocrisy and imposition—all having in view the easy elevation, through craft, to power and luxurious ease, of the non-laboring classes. And melancholy is indeed the fact that the laboring classes have often lent themselves to these arts of designing men, and contributed to their own degradation. And it is the greatest political revolution yet to be effected, to bring the laboring man to know that honest industry is the highest of merit, and should be awarded the highest honor, and properly pursued contributes to his intelligence and morality, and to the virtues needed for official station.

Without analysing the relation between labor and its productive means, it will be readily seen, that where no tyrannical measures are adopted to furnish a favored class with means, at the expense of the laborers, all, or nearly all, must labor for a living, and where labor is duly honored, and this great laboring class elevated, not only is great happiness gained to the community, but corresponding wealth; for, industry being a merit, it will be pursued with laudable zeal, to the production of means, or wealth.

On the other hand, where labor is despised, and the laborer degraded and held to believe his position inevitably connected with meanness and misery, not only is the laboring class, which must still be a great majority in the community, made unhappy, but labor being degrading, all, who can, will avoid labor as a means of living, and thus reduce productiveness or wealth, both through the want of zeal in the laborer, and the withdrawal of many from occupations of labor, who will resort to artifices and clandestine means of living rather than laboring; such is unfortunately too much our present condition. A further point to be noticed, is the vice engendered, both by the degradation of the laborers, and the idleness and craft of the non-laborers. To the reader who has followed us thus far we would make an application of these views upon the question of slavery in the territories.

In countries where slavery exists, labor devolves there for the most part upon the slaves, and is therefore identified with slavery; and the white free laborer being valued by slaveowners, who control public opinion, only as so much physical organism (bone, muscle, &c.) for producing means, he is degraded to the condition of the slave, so far as his influence and moral status go, and is even lower in physical comforts, for the want of the intelligent care the slaveowner bestows upon the slave, and of which he, the free laborer, has become incompetent by a mental depravity corresponding to his moral degradation. This is a truth of philosophy and political economy, that man rises to a position corresponding to the rights and responsibilities devolved upon him, and therefore the only true way to make a man is to invest him with the rights, duties, and responsibilities of a man, and he generally rises in intellectual and moral greatness to a position corresponding to these circumstances; and it is the very want of them that makes the free non-slaveholding persons of the slave states so degraded and imbecile that the slaves themselves feel a conscious superiority, in which they are encouraged by their owners, to the extent of thinking it better to be a nigger than a poor white man; and this is done to pacify the slave, and thus secure this artificial system of securing the products of labor to the non-laboring classes, and also, by degrading white laborers, prevent their industry from competing with slave labor to reduce thereby the value of slaves.

So true are these things, that it is well known that the poor whites of the slave states are the most subservient tools of the slaveowners, and that of all the artificial systems devised by tyranny to impose upon the poor man, none have anywhere reduced him to such squalid poverty and utterly degraded demoralization as prevail among the free laborers of the slave states. Such is the state of things which, with the Dred Scott decision and the policy of the Democracy, scourged on by the lash of its southern masters, we are to have not only in Kansas, but all our territories. For this purpose is a slave code to be imposed against the will of our people, Kansas to be kept in territorial bondage, the Homestead Bill to be defeated, and the whole power and patronage of the government prostituted to the purpose of opposing the intellectual, moral, and physical development of the industrial classes, whose energetic resources have in hand at once the welfare both of themselves and our country, and the uprooting of slavery in the territories.

To this cause we are unalterably committed; such is our platform and the purpose of our candidate. Upon our candidate we must omit in this article, on account of its length, the points which controlled his nomination and render him the fit exponent of our principles, in view of which, and the ready acquiescence of all the great competitors (some of whom must have, in any event, been disappointed), we have no hesitation upon our course of duty.

Our principles, as above given, make Abe Lincoln a more suitable candidate, perhaps, than could have been well otherwise selected, as his present greatness and position are due to the operation of the great principles we now advocate for our Territories—that of honoring labor and elevating the honest laborer, of whom we intend, in this case, to make our next President.

June 9, 1860.

II.

OUR CAUSE—OUR CANDIDATE.

In our former article under this head, we showed our cause to be more distinctly that of elevating the free laborer, by keeping him from contact with the system of slave labor, by which he is reduced, in moral status, to a level with, or lower than that of the slave. That honest industry is in no way inconsistent with high intellectual culture and moral elevation, is shown by the condition of the generality of our laborers in the free states, and such examples as Benjamin Franklin, N. P. Banks, and our distinguished candidate for the presidency, Abraham Lincoln. That this is the reverse in the slave states, we proved, not only from the nature of the case, but the existing condition of the free laborer there, where he is so much demoralized as to be inoffensive to the oligarchists of the slave interest, who control the political machinery of their respective states, so as to make all things harmonize with, or subservient to this interest. And by a shrewd foresight and combination, in conjunction with unscrupulous leaders north, they are attempting, through the machinery of the general government, to extend this system over our free territories.

It is not our purpose to consider, further than is incidental to the subject of slavery in the territories, the effects of slavery upon the owners of slaves, their social and political economy; as by our platform, founded upon the fact of the existence of slavery in the southern states at the period of our political compacts, we bind ourselves to adhere to all moral obligations involved therein, and refrain from any hostilities towards the institution of slavery in those states. This we shall do; but as incident to the question of slavery in the territories, we have illustrated its degrading effects upon the free laborer, and now further warn our brethren against contributing to build up, in our midst, an oligarchy of proud, domineering slaveowners, so lamented and graphically described by Jefferson, and whose position and interests place them in antagonism to the free laborer, whom they despise and denounce as they did in the last presidential election through the southern press, as "greasy mechanics," "filthy operatives," &c. We quote:

"Free society is a monstrous abortion, and slavery the healthy, beautiful, and natural being, which they are trying, unconsciously, to adopt. The slaves are governed far better than the free laborers at the north are governed. Our negroes are not only better off as to physical comforts than are those free laborers, but their moral condition is better."

Such may be indeed the condition of the free laborers at the south, and these views of the Richmond *Enquirer* are founded upon this condition, and they establish by southern authority the points we have advanced—the arrogance, on the one hand, of the slaveowner, and the degradation on the other, of the free laborer. Again:—

"Free society! we sicken at the name! What is it but a conglomeration of greasy mechanics, filthy operatives, small-fisted farmers, and moonstruck theorists? All the northern, and especially the New England States, are devoid of society fitted for a well-bred gentleman. The prevailing class one meets with is that of mechanics struggling to be genteel, and small farmers who do their own drudgery, and yet they are hardly fit for a gentleman's body servant. This is your free society, which your northern hordes are endeavoring to extend into Kansas."

Yes, and if we can attain the standard of New England, here cited for condemnation by the Muscogee *Herald* (Ala.), we shall be satisfied. How far we are to stultify our own interests, integrity, and common-sense, by sustaining the Democracy, and thereby contributing, through the general government, to make ourselves subject to, and sustain this garrulous abuse of us, we are glad of the opportunity soon to show.

> "A man's a man for a' that,
> The honest man, tho' e'er sae poor,
> Is king o' men for a' that.
> Then let us pray that come it may,
> And come it will for a' that,
> That sense and worth, o'er a' the earth,
> May bear the gree and a' that.
> That man to man the world o'er,
> Shall brothers be for a' that."
>
> BURNS'S *Honest Poverty.*

Our worthy candidate is an illustration of these lofty sentiments of the immortal poet, and this we trust will be more fully shown, to the confusion of our arch-enemy, in his presidential capacity.

A word now upon this part of our heading— *Our Candidate.* Mr. Seward was the strongest man before the Chicago convention, and had probably friends enough in it who preferred him, to have given him the nomination, but of whom, many having the cause of Republicanism more at heart than the elevation of their favorite, feared his availability, on account of his supposed affection for and affiliation with northern abolitionists, as have been charged, for a long time past, by his opponents, on account of his past political views and acts, and more especially his late " irrepressible conflict" doctrine. And though ill-founded, these charges were liable to hurt Mr. Seward with many of our conservative and life-long democratic Republicans, with whom Mr. Seward is not a favorite. Mr. Seward also hurt himself with his Republican friends, we think, in supporting the President's policy of a military regimen over Kansas, as he did, by voting to raise new troops for the Utah service (against the Mormons), and thereby enable the army, then in Kansas, to remain there.

Let us not be understood as disparaging Mr. Seward, nor withholding gratitude for his eminent services, but, as is well said by the New York *Evening Post*, what Mr. Seward is and has been he attained through the approbation of the people, and it becomes him and his friends to accept, and be satisfied with such approbation as the people see fit to manifest, and is valuable only as it is bestowed unsolicited, without management or force. Mr. Seward readily acquiesces, as we know, and cordially we believe —his friends, no doubt, will also.

To our four friends from Ohio, McLean, Chase, Wade and Corwin, whom we name in the order of our preferences, we have less objections on the score of qualifications and availability, than the fact, that being all from the same State, where each has deservedly warm friends, heartburnings and jealousies might arise at the triumph of one over the other rivals, whereby a coolness towards the one selected, might endanger success in a State we cannot well spare.

Mr. Bates was popular, but it must be borne in mind that he is a late acquisition to our ranks, and though one of which we are proud, he has not struggled with us in our days of darkness and trial, but on the contrary, in the last Presidential election, when the wail of our sufferings touched every sympathetic heart, Mr. Bates joined the diversion made by Mr. Fillmore in favor of the Democrats, which caused our defeat. His nomination, we have reason to fear, would have hurt us with our naturalized citizens, who, if true to themselves, in the advocacy of their own elevation, will prove an important element and efficient aid towards the attainment of our cause.

Mr. Banks is a man of ability and pure patriotism, and had our confidence, but we make no lamentations over a result, in which almost every one having a favorite candidate must be disappointed. But we are gratified to see, that the friends of the eminent men above named, and of others like Clay, Blair, Foote, Collamer, &c., under the examples of their respective favorites, are all united to support the nominee of the Chicago convention. This nominee, ABRAHAM LINCOLN, now stands before the country as our standard-bearer, than whom none could have been more happily chosen, as the embodiment of our great cause of the laboring man. His stalwart frame, honest heart, and comprehensive, well-trained mind, confound the sneering taunts of the slave oligarchy at free labor, and point to us, with unerring certainty, the pathway of duty, which shall lead to our highest humanity, from which we shall gaze with a mournful smile, at the impotent jeers of the proud and vain, who follow their blind infatuation to a shameful end.

June 16, 1860.

III.

OUR CAUSE—OUR CANDIDATE.

In our last article under this head, we gave reasons why many of the leading competitors were not nominated at the Chicago Convention, and it follows by consequence that the nomination must fall upon Mr. Lincoln if others could not get it. But this would leave our nominee in the negative position of owing success to being unobjectionable, rather than commanding support from commendable attributes and character. But it was well known to all in Chicago at the time, and the history of the Convention shows that Mr. Lincoln was among the foremost at the start, and it was due to the hold his commendable qualities had upon his friends in Convention, that they, joined by the overwhelming outside pressure in the city and State, were enabled to secure the success of their favorite candidate. "Give us, Lincoln," said Illinois, "and you shall have our vote—we gave it to him as a state for the United States Senate against Douglas—our popular majority for him in that canvass is the foundation of this confidence." This is enough to show how Mr. Lincoln stands where he is best known. He had, however, his share of public life in the Legislature of his own State, and as member of Congress, and it is not too much to say, that he always justified the support awarded him, by executing the trusts committed to his charge. It is this fidelity to his own principles, and the interests with which he has been entrusted, more than anything else that has controlled this nomination—a nomination made more appropriate by the sad disappointment of the country at the falseness of the Democracy to every profession and political creed.

It is not our purpose here to give a biography of Mr. Lincoln, showing the steps by which he rose, through industry and integrity, as so many of our countrymen have done, to successive positions of trust and honor; but that he has so risen, against every disadvantage in youth, to his present position, which commands the confidence, and constitutes the hope of the great Republican party, is the main feature in his qualifications for our candidate, at this period when the sole tangible issue between us and the Democracy is, this very question of elevating the honest and poor laborer through industry—whether that industry, which is the parent of virtue and means of all material happiness, shall be held in respect, as we urge, to the elevation and happiness of the vast laboring classes and the great increase of wealth in the country, as is mainly the case in our free States, though not to the extent we desire; or whether, as urged by the Democracy, labor, being made to rest upon a basis of slavery, industry or all engaged in it must be held in degradation and despised by a self-constituted oligarchy, invested with the possession and control of labor.

That this is the impending issue we have shown in our previous articles on this subject, and it is lamentable, that the morbid desire of man to overreach the laborer, and make his productiveness subservient to his convenience, has, through artful devices, so imposed upon the laborer as to secure his own co-operation to this end. Such we think has, in times gone by, been more or less the case in the artful schemes of party to build up a privileged class, founded on property in banks, manufactories, &c., while it was more obviously so, in the support given, at the last Presidential election, to the so-called Democracy, which had in view, and it is now so seen, the building up of an aristocracy founded on property in "niggers."

Thus was the Honorable Jefferson Davis right in saying in the Senate the other day, that the Democratic party had taken the place of the old Whig party, for so it has, in the feature formerly attributed to the Whig party, of desiring to build up a select class of privileged persons, to obtain their means, through special legislation, at the expense of the industrial classes.

This morbid desire for wealth and power, this bane of the human heart, rises, hydra-like, in every place and shape to tempt the weak and blind, and mislead the strong, and unfortunately has, at different times, lured Man with its syren songs to the fatal embrace of tyranny, in which the history of the world has so generally found him. Against this we now war, and with the more earnestness, as with the artfulness of a deity, and the presumption of a fiend, our own Constitution is perversely claimed, by the Democracy, as the ægis for the establishment of this slave autocracy over our country. We thus again advert to this struggle so artfully though vainly pursued, between aristocracy, or capital, and labor, in order to show more fully the fitness of our candidate, as a laboring man, and one who has risen by industry from obscurity and indigence to carry on the great work which, through so many hard-fought battles, has so satisfactorily progressed in this country, towards placing the honest laborer on that just eminence, which the wants of society and the laws of nature demand, and so imperiously demand, that any artificial system which blinks or ignores them, must be ever subject to unhappy changes and revolutions; and it may be safely asserted, that this is at the foundation of all disturbances in society. We commend our friends to the history of our candidate to learn his fitness upon our great national issues.

Nor must we omit a reference to our candidate for the Vice-Presidency, whose well-known modesty and integrity, combined with his high moral courage and eminence as a statesman, make Hannibal Hamlin, of Maine, fit for any position, and the most honorable acquisition to our ticket. As Senator he could not violate his conscience to vote, under instructions, for the repeal of the Missouri Compromise, and thereupon resigned his seat and returned home, to co-operate in establishing the principles of Republicanism in his State, upon which he became Governor, and soon returned to the Senate, where he now is, an honor to that body, and, as an illustration of the triumphs of integrity, a bright example to his race, among whom none can be found of purer thoughts or loftier emotions, than those now animating the peaceful heart and irradiating the genial brow of Hannibal Hamlin.

O ye who would know man as man and a brother, who, true to yourselves, would respond to the aspirations of those whose lives are devoted to our cause, we beacon you to the standard which now floats the illustrious names of Lincoln and Hamlin, inscribed there with the cause of free labor, beneath the folds of which we glow with joy for the fight, in which we will engage, so long as man has the weakness, to suffer or tyranny the power to strike.

June 23, 1860.

IV.

SOVEREIGN SQUATTEREIGNTY.

We prefer to advocate our principles and win support for them by their own commendable features, rather than expose and denounce the detestable iniquities of our opponents, for the purpose of creating an aversion towards them.

For this reason the contemptible cant of Black Republicanism, negro worshippers, &c., applied to us, have passed unheeded as the loathsome spew of the envenomed Shamocracy, which we leave to the intelligent to perceive, and that our advocacy of the interests of the great laboring classes arises from the principles, that whatever contributes to our welfare permanently is the true element towards the substantial happiness of all, and ultimately of the negro. Because slavery has evils which we oppose extending into territories, an attempt is made to attach odium to us, by representing us as abolitionists, who are understood to insist upon the abolition of slavery at once, and without regard to consequences, with a view to the welfare of the slave, and under a fanatical sense of moral obligations to pursue this course. We oppose slavery in the territories, not for a love of the negro but the white man, whom we would save from the condition, either as an arrogant slaveholder, or as degraded by him, in which we find him in the slave states. Nor do we want the free blacks, for, degraded as they are, they constitute a pernicious element, like other unfortunate subjects of society—the depraved and foolish —and our confidence is, that the attainment of our welfare will carry that of theirs also.

But it may be pertinent, under present circumstances, to call attention to the practical workings of the great hobby of our opponents, called "Squatter Sovereignty," or, as illustrated by its apostle, Douglas, is more properly defined, as in our heading, "Sovereign Squattereignty." Some six years ago, while the country was in profound quiet over the subject of slavery, resting upon the security of the compromises made in regard to it, Mr. Douglas convulsed the country upon the right of the people of a territory to vote slavery into that portion from which it has been prohibited by the Missouri Compromise of 1820. This, under a great hue and cry that the people possessed absolute sway, and had a right to legislate in the territories, for or against slavery, in the same manner as upon other property, ardent spirits, &c.

The Republicans make issue this far, that it is the right and duty of Congress to interfere and prevent the few, who first reach a territory, from forestalling the sentiments of the larger community, likely to occupy it, and should, therefore protect all classes of people, in their infant state, against premature and grasping assumptions, as in the case of the Mormons in Utah, and the border ruffians in Kansas. The Kansas-Nebraska Bill was framed with the most liberal provisions for the rights of the people, with the evident design that these rights were to be used, under Government direction, to introduce slavery; but, nevertheless, these rights were invested in the people of the Territory, and a due regard to the terms of the law as well as the moral obligations involved, should have secured to the people the exercise of this right; and when, by the inroads of border ruffians, sanctioned and aided by Government officials, they were deprived of this right and subjected to most oppressive tyranny, in palpable violation of the terms and spirit of the law, Mr. Stephen Arnold Douglas, so far from sympathizing with them, repudiates the principles of his own bill, and joins our southern enemies in the most violent denunciation of us, and urges the penalty of treason upon those who oppose the revolting tyranny of border ruffianism. Exulting in the power of these Kansas inroads, he would unite that of the General Government, over the people, and in support of the Toombs' Bill provide for a commission to be appointed by the corrupt executive, who had lent himself to these oppressions, which commission was to provide a State government, irrespective of the will of the people. And when at length the people assert their rights under the Territorial Bill, Mr. Douglas readily repudiates his own doctrine, by acquiescing in the Dred Scott decision of the Supreme Court, annulling all this pretended right of the people over the subject of slavery, in the territories, showing that all this clamor, for the people's rights, was but the deceptive art of the demagogue.

He stands beside Senator Sumner and witnesses the inhuman attack upon him, without a lisp or act of remonstrance, for fear of affronting the South. This may be "Squatter Sovereignty" with Mr. Douglas and his friends, but, in extent of prostitution to the demands of the slave power, we do not see how he can squat lower, or become more literally a "*Sovereign Squatter.*" The *squat* of the duck, in a thunder-storm, serves but a weak illustration of the humiliating depth to which Mr. Douglas has gone in the slime of his own putrescence, before the flash and roar of his southern masters.

It is true, the last Presidential election developed an opposing storm, before which he fain would squat to the attainment of his end, could he rise against that to which he had before succumbed. This he partially did in his Lecompton issue, and a courageous struggle, persistently pursued, might have enabled him to regain a safe shelter, but timidity again arouses morbid apprehensions from the overcharged storm on the John Brown raid, and again he squats to his meanest depths before the southern blasts. We, of course, allude to his scurrilous abuse of us, in his speech upon measures of redress for such occurrences as that of Harper's Ferry, and the severity, too revolting even for slaveholders to accept, with which he proposed to furnish them. The consternation of the duck or toad in a thunder-storm is sweet tranquillity compared to the distress, under these circumstances, of our "sovereign squatter." You have "squat" too low, my dear sir, in the mire beneath your feet, and the unceasing storm, centring its fury upon you, shall keep you there. Palsied at the time, you could not raise a helping hand for a brother Senator, sinking beneath its blows. We now leave you to the impotent struggles with an overwhelming fate to which your morbid ambition, overriding your discretion, has reduced you.

Quitting this mortifying spectacle, of "Sovereign Squattereignty," we turn with joy to the bright hopes of Republicanism, which requires no spurious oracles nor juggler's arts to command for it our affections.

June 30, 1860.

V.

ARE WE SUBDUED?

"We will subdue you," was the declaration of the British ministry to our petitioners for redress of grievances upon which our forefathers warred successfully to the confusion of the insolent authors of this impotent threat. "We will subdue you," was the language of Stephen A. Douglas to the people of Kansas, when remonstrating against the oppressive tyranny of the border ruffian rule; and the present state of our people shows this oracle of the southern oligarchy to have been about as prophetic as that of their monarchical prototype.

Presuming upon the power of their government, on the one hand, and the feebleness of the colonies on the other, our illustrious Franklin, who had gone to the mother country to represent the wrongs done the American colonies, and upon what terms a reconciliation could be effected, and by which alone a revolution could be averted, was dismissed by the British ministry from this mission with scurrilous abuse to himself, and the threat to his people—"We will subdue you,"—"We will ravage your whole country, lay your seaport towns in ashes," &c. "My property," replied Franklin, "consists of houses in these towns. Of these, indeed, you may make bonfires and reduce them to ashes, but the fear of losing them will never alter my resolution to resist, to the last, the claims of Parliament." The sacrifices of the Kansas people, under similar threats, show them, happily, not destitute of similar heroic virtues.

Benedict Arnold becomes a traitor to these principles, and after attempting to betray the interests with which he had been entrusted, he heads a party of our enemies and goes forth against his own people and native state, with the motto, "We will subdue you," to ravage the country, lay seaport towns in ashes, &c.; and the burning of New London and massacre at Fort Griswold are well known results of his leadership, emblematic, in their unutterable cruelty, of the ineffable debasement of treachery.

Stephen Arnold Douglas—and by what a singular coincidence is the name *Arnold* here appropriately found, and becomes so prominent that he is now generally called *Arnold Douglas*—in a similar manner betrays the principles he had advocated in behalf of the rights of the people to self-government, and relying upon the power of the government, and the weak, distressed condition of what he denominates " Kansas Shrickers," he denounces them in scurrilous language, and demands, as the oracle of the pro-slavery faction, then dominant over the Pierce administration, that they shall submit tamely to the border-ruffian rule; and when remonstrated with, and told that revolution must soon follow, and that no fear of consequences could alter their " resolution to resist, to the last, the claims " so oppressive, he flashes an embodiment of rage, raising himself up with clenched hands, shakes his shaggy head, gesticulating with fierceness, strikes his desk, and stamping with violence his feet, exclaims, " *We will subdue you!* " Arnold like—as he is—he now heads our enemies, and sets forth against his own people; and the atrocity upon Senator Sumner, and the murders and massacres of Kansas, under the subduing process, are well known results of this arrogant spirit, and to be traced, more or less, to the moral effect of his leadership.

The lessons of Lord North and Benedict

Arnold had been taught in vain for him; but he learns at last, in that dear school where fools will only learn, that we are not to be subdued. A little bit further parallel may be drawn from history. The battle of Stillwater and the espousal by France of our cause, brought Lord North to doubt the success of the subduing process, and then, too late, he proposed to relinquish it. The battle of the last Presidential election, and the effective sympathy for Kansas, has made this aspiring ape of tyranny hesitate in his subjugating career, and, too late, he now proposes reconciliation. His course, like that of Lord North, gains the sympathy of a few forgiving friends, who now assume his fervent meekness as proof of untainted purity. And this is the basis of merit to the support of which our aid is now invoked! Ah, Arnold Douglas! Arnold Benedict had a history, and the events of it cannot be effaced from the memory and indignation of an injured people; nor, sir, will the prominent events of your history fail of proper resentment, so long as shame and outrage inflame the manly bosom or rouse the manly frame.

July 14, 1860.

VI.

THE MORAL OF THE QUESTION.

In ascertaining our relations to the world around us, we find by our observation and experience, and by precept, transmitting the wisdom of preceding ages, that certain rules and regulations are necessary for our welfare and happiness. Some of these rules apply to ourselves, in our individual capacity, to regulate our habits of diet, sleep, industry, amusements, &c., and others to our social relations, and regulate our intercourse with those around us.

Of these rules, such as contribute to our own welfare and happiness, and that of the community in general, are called Morals, and constitute the code of morals in contradistinction to those which are pernicious, and are called vices, and constitute crimes. Upon this view, whatever contributes most to our welfare and that of the community— and so interwoven are our own interests with those of society, that whatever we do for one is necessarily done for the other—is the highest of morals; and, therefore, as has been well said by our best of philosophers, we need no other rule for our guidance than that of "our own self-love, that universal principle of action."

And if in pursuing this rule, we secure our substantial and permanent welfare, this welfare will of necessity manifest itself in some physical advancement and advantages, and our standard of morality may therefore be assumed to be that course of conduct which, in the long run, contributes most to our physical wealth and prosperity.

Under the vicious system, spring irregularities, suffering, and misery, and finally weakness and decay, till on the verge of despair the subjects of it either sink and expire, both individually and socially, or, by reform, avail themselves of the moral regimen, and return to prosperity and happiness.

The history of the world is full of the ups and downs of individuals and of nations under the operations of these laws—prosperity begetting presumption, arrogance, and a disregard of the moral law, till a consequent suffering effects premature death, or impels reform and relief. New nations, societies, and clans, being at first weak, usually, on initiating their organizations and institutions, adopt strictly the moral code, and by this means, more than by any inherent virtues of this system, prosper for a time, till pride and presumption follow with countervailing effects.

Our own national existence affords an illustration of these views. Correct or moral in the administration of our laws at home, and our intercourse with other nations, our people were contented and loyal, and through these means our government strong; while with our neighbors amicable and disarmed of malice, we were secure from harm abroad. Modest and subdued from our toils and sufferings, and industrious from our poverty, our people and country rose in wealth, power, and popularity, and all eyes turned in wonder and admiration upon so worthy an example for observation and imitation.

But a metamorphosis now interposes—while we have lost none of the elements of our prosperity, we find discordance and din throughout our land—discontent at home and disgrace abroad. Government, with the fatuity of James II., wars upon the sacred popular rights of our people, to obtrude an obnoxious institution over a people who refuse to admit it, and, with revolting disregard of moral obligations, involves us in turpitude, with covertly lending itself to the slave trade, and fillibustering schemes against our neighbors. A long standing compact, which had formed an adjustment of otherwise irreconcilable differences on the slavery question, is ruthlessly torn asunder, in utter disregard and contempt of the wishes of one of the parties to it, and border-ruffian rule stalks unrestrained, with iron heels, over the fair surface of Kansas, leaving behind the lurid clouds of slavery.

Stung with mortification, and enraged at these events, uprose our masses, who, after several confused manifestations of feelings, have settled into the compact and effective organization of the Republican party. An appeal is now made in behalf of slavery and the outrages which have characterized the attempt to extend it, to this great party of opposition to the wrongs and rapacity of the Democracy, upon the ground of our dogma, with which we set out, that morals conduce to physical benefits; and the converse, that whatever is highly and permanently beneficial is therefore moral. For it is said (and we admit it), let our sophisms be what they may, let perverse theories of morals arise upon innumerably contested theological points, all must settle down to, and acquiesce in, those physical results which secure us the greatest wealth and happiness. And as slavery constitutes the wealth of the South, and the proceeds of slave labor have lately enriched it much, and enhanced, through its production of cotton, rice, tobacco, &c., the wealth and happiness of the civilized world, therefore slavery is the normal state of society in morals, and consequent physical results. Therefore is it a pious duty to maintain it where it is, and a blessing to extend it; and plighted faith broken, a sacred compact annulled, and obligations to honor disregarded, are but the needful and excusable sacrifice to so philanthropic an object.

The sudden rise in the value of labor, from the opening of the California mines, and of the price of cotton, from the increased demand for it for emigrant and mining life, army service, and on our ships of commerce, have given undoubted advancement to the wealth of the slave states, and to the value of the slave, and this sudden and unexpected rise from dilapidation and poverty, has led to the erroneous presumption of merit and advantage in the institution of slavery. For, though circumstances have combined to increase the prosperity of the South, the North has availed herself of her superior industry and enterprise, to develop her wealth to a degree more than corresponding to that of the South, and she, as well as other portions of the civilized world, still have comparatively the moral advantage, upon the standard of physical effects, by which she must still loathe slavery, as of her old and former aspect—the superinducing cause of misery and poverty.

With the patrons of the system, upon the standard of morals and of physical effects, we have only to deal so far as in Congress and the operations of the General Government (now unfortunately under their control) their influence is felt.

How that influence has been exerted, was shown to some extent, not long since, as we mentioned, by the investigations of the Covode Committee, and the exhibition may be well left to an intelligent people to judge of the morally elevating effects of the slave system, and how far an appeal for the further extension of it commends itself to their judgment.

July 21, 1860.

VII.

THE MORAL OF THE QUESTION.

In our former article, under this head, we considered the morals of slavery under the new and recent claim set up for it, that, as an element of essential prosperity and wealth to the South, it must be accepted as of moral character, because of its beneficial physical effects. If the recent improvement of the South, from the great rise in cotton and price of labor, though less in degree than that at the North, has made any converts to the system, they are welcome to their new faith, and we ask no co-operation for our cause from persons of such easy virtue. But this is a pretext on the part of the slave interest, to justify the position they have attained in the control of the national government, through artifice on their part and subserviency of Northern doughfaces.

At first, under the general disapprobation of

the Fathers of the Republic, and the execration of the civilized world, the slave interest sought shelter and excuse under a plea of having been unavoidably imposed and submitted to, and appealed to the magnanimity of our national association for its toleration. Not only has this toleration been free and unstinted, but security of it confirmed in our national organization, and subsequent operations of the national government. Though slavery formerly existed in nearly all the States, such was the opposition to it at the North, that great concessions were required on her part to the relations that must arise from its existence in the Union. The generosity of this concession and faithful adherence to it have, in times gone by, had their happy effects in mutual confidence and good-will between the two sections of our country. But uneasy and aspiring men South, affect alarm at the ranting of a few insane abolitionists at the North, and presuming upon the generosity of the North, clamor for such an enunciation of principles as shall suit their wishes, on the part of the party, North, to which they shall give their support. Though not united at first in this scheme it has become so, and is now the leading policy of Southern statesmen, and with the aid of a few Northern mercenaries such has been their success, that from affecting fear for the safety of slavery they now exact a national support of it, and require of their candidate for the Presidency, a pledge to use his influence for this purpose, and, as the most satisfactory evidence of his fidelity, that he shall give most of the offices under the Government to Southern men. A notable instance, under this head, has recently transpired. Our readers must have noticed the death of Gen. Jessup of the army—a man of eminence and ability—who, in dying, left vacant the position he held, at the head of his corps, as Quartermaster-General of the Army. The next officer in rank to him in the Quartermaster's corps—a corps composed of Colonels, Lieut.-Colonels, Majors, and Captains—was Colonel Thomas of Pennsylvania, who being in regular order of promotion, and fitted for it, was promised the vacancy by the President, who, it is said, held out this promise to the latest moment. But alas! Colonel Thomas is not from a slave State, and a doughface Northern President must show his soundness on the goose, and his subserviency to Southern demands by giving this appointment to one who is. Colonel Johnson, of Virginia, is the man, and, as understood, a fit appointment enough, except the motives to it, and the cruel disregard of others eligibly entitled to it; if he were from the North, he would have no rights under the Government. This instance is mentioned, only as a recent and prominent one, of the success under the present and past administrations of the South in controlling the Government and Government appointments, upon the eternal cry of "Nigger"—a stock of political capital which we believe to be well nigh exhausted. The monopoly of Government appointments by the South, is, of course, well known, and the application of Government money to secure votes and the election of Northern men to subserve Southern interests has been partially shown by the Covode Committee in Congress. Our Secretary of the Navy figures largely in corrupt contracts for building vessels, furnishing coal, hands, etc., and due investigations into other departments would doubtless have made equally unpleasant exposures. Our exquisite Army Secretary has already figured conspicuously in the Fort Snelling sale, and Willett's Point purchase, and we have learned of several transactions of like venality. The purchases of horses and mules for the Utah Army was let out to contractors (who of course wore the right colors on the slavery question) at enormous rates, and who sublet at about half these rates. Soon after these animals reached Utah, a mania for economy prompts our loyal Secretary to direct a prompt sale of them, on so short a notice and such arbitrary conditions, that only some favored confidants and capitalists can purchase, and upon being thus sold at a great sacrifice, are again repurchased by the Government in Oregon. The firm of Major & Russell had a monopolizing contract to carry supplies to Utah, and a large army kept there gives them a large business and corresponding profits, but on losing this business this year, by being underbid, and getting that for New Mexico, the troops are at once transferred to this latter place, leaving Utah nearly vacant, while both the Secretary and President admit that the Mormons will again presume upon the weakness of Government authority there, to renew open hostility to it. Our troops here upon our Indian border, and upon whom our safety depends against the hostile Kiowas and Camanches hovering near us, are, we have just learned, ordered to a different station to swell the flow of business-profits for the Major & Russell firm.

Corn, we see by advertisements, is to be furnished these distant posts per transportation of this firm from Kansas City, when in our vicinity, at from one hundred and fifty to two hundred miles nearer, plenty of corn can be had at a saving of half the cost at Kansas City, and the price of transportation for this distance. This business transacted here would save one hundred per cent. to the Government, and greatly relieve our community, so much in want of a market. True, our people are not sound on the goose, but we regret this must involve so much loss to Government. We have heard of such things before, but not felt them at our doors. A contractor was allowed to furnish flour in Utah, at cost in Leavenworth, and price of transportation added, which would make it rate some $28 per one hundred pounds, but who purchased there on the spot, at from $6 to $8 per one hundred pounds, and thereby realized over some $20 per one hundred pounds upon his contract.

If slavery engenders this spirit, or exacts of government such practices in its behalf, we shall hardly become adherents to the standard of morals claimed for it.

July 28, 1860.

VIII.

TRUE TO HIS MISSION.

Squatter sovereignty, or the sovereignty of the people in the territories over their domestic affairs, including slavery, has been the affected hobby of Mr. Douglas, though in practice, as we have before shown in our columns, the readiness with which he abandons every principle that would give efficacy to that term, renders him a squatter in the mire of self-humiliation, and this hobby one of sovereign squattereignty. This was seen in his ready acquiescence in the border ruffian and federal executive tyranny over Kansas, in violation of the squatter sovereignty doctrines in the Toombs' Bill, which scorned it, and in the Dred Scott decision, which annihilates every vestige of it.

To render the whole power and patronage of the Government subservient to the interests of the slaveholders, and struggling with a resolution and desperation peculiar to his character, is, and ever has been, the true mission of Mr. Douglas; and that he will never swerve from it we think evident to all who have observed his direct purpose but tortuous course to this end.

When the sentiment of the country was so averse to slavery that Missouri was denied, for two years, admission to the Union, because her constitution provided for slavery, she finally came in on condition that the country west of her should never have slavery. Mr. Douglas, in looking back upon the trick by which a slave State is acquired, glories over it, and rejoices in the sacredness of the binding contract, "akin to the constitution, which no ruthless hand will ever be reckless enough to disturb."

Texas is admitted, and he affects fairness towards the North, by resolving that slavery shall not exist north of 36-30, which was the Missouri compromise line. Bear in mind this line now has, with him, no constitutional objections. Our conquests from Mexico must next have their adjustment upon the slavery issue. California was already demanding admission as a free State, and, the more justly, clamorous, because the slave question has prevented the provision for her of a territorial government.

Utah, under the name of Deseret, was in the same condition; and New Mexico preparing to take the same attitude. General Taylor, then President, seizing upon these features, recommended them to the favor of Congress as the best method of avoiding the angry contest over slavery. This would never do; Mr. Douglas, fearing the favor of public sentiment, which required the application of the proviso against slavery, introduced by Mr. Wilmot, and since called the Wilmot proviso, again invokes the efficacy of the Missouri compromise line, against which no constitutional scruples now arise, excusing himself to the South that this is the best that he can do, as it is the only alternative of the Wilmot proviso. Finally, the territories were organized upon the basis of ignoring the subject of slavery, till, on becoming a state, the people were to provide for or against slavery, as they should see fit.

Kansas now seems to offer herself an easy prey to the cupidity of the slaveholders of Missouri, who being settled upon, and within her boundary, assured our pro-slavery missionary they could easily control this subject, if the Missouri compromise restriction were removed. This he sets about and accomplishes, raising himself the hand he had characterized as ruthless, to disturb a compact which, so long as it served pro-slavery purposes, was to be regarded as "canonized in the hearts of the American people," &c., but which, now that it restrains such purposes, must be recklessly torn asunder. Kansas is so framed as to be made an easy victim; instead of having half of the newly organized Territory, Nebraska is given the most of it, and her northern boundary kept somewhat below that of Missouri, in order to be within the Missouri influence, and to prevent contact with the free State of Iowa. A further precaution in favor of slavery is to leave out a strip of half a degree in width on the South, so that if by chance Kansas should become free, this might still stand a chance for slavery.

How he hated and despised Kansas for her efforts at freedom, and how under the cry, "We will subdue you," he opposed her, we have before mentioned, and is too nauseous a subject to bear more than an allusion to here.

And now comes on the stage the Native American party—then called Know-Nothings, and for stupidity of purpose a very appropriate name—which party suddenly overwhelmed many parts of the country, and carried into Congress so many members that it held there a balance of power, and for a long time prevented the election of a Speaker of the House.

It is easily seen that this party is of necessity pro-slavery; its candidate is avowedly so, and as it opposes the emigration and settlement here of persons of foreign birth, it would thus, as far as possible, check the flood of free laborers to the West, and keep it and all our unoccupied territory in a condition for easier competition on the part of the pro-slavery powers. It is indeed this very element of free labor, and elevated laborers, that is to give the final blow to slavery everywhere, and nothing therefore is more natural to the pro-slavery man than to resort to his usual artifice, coeval with weakness and wickedness, to arouse a prejudice against our foreign population, in order to prevent their accession to this element. Under the subtle and specious disguise of devotion to Americans, enough of northern Republicans were hoodwinked to keep Mr. Banks for a long time out of the Speaker's chair, and finally to defeat Mr. Fremont for the Presidency. True to their instincts and the purpose of their mission, the Douglas Democrats, who have played no other part than to subserve Southern interests, and invent and palm off ingenious, but poor excuses, to the North, find Mr. Aiken's native Americanism so congenial to their purposes, that he gets their whole vote and comes within one of as many votes as Mr. Banks for the speakership.

So indignant is Mr. Douglas that some members of the American party from the North voted for Mr. Banks, that while he denounces the Northern portion of it, he assures us at the same time, as Mr. Crittenden and others, that his terms do not apply to the Americans South. Americanism North was offensive, but modified at the South with pro-slavery sentiments, it is so acceptable that his party from the North can come in a body to the support for speakership of the American member from South Carolina.

The same thing was continually repeated last winter in the contest for Speakership in which the Douglas party supported American members from the South, in order to defeat Sherman and Pennington. A. R. Boteler of Va., W. N. H. Smith and J. A. Gilmer of N. C., H. Maynard of Tenn., and others were so supported. Mr. Douglas struggles hard to conciliate Northern men, under the idea that he does not make the extension of slavery and its protection in the territories a political creed, and is, in this respect, separated from, and an object of persecution by, his political associates South, who have Mr. Breckenridge as an opposing candidate for the presidency.

Following him in his subtle windings, we find him still undeviating from his first love, and desperate as ever in his plottings to secure the ascendency of the pro-slavery party at every sacrifice of self and self-interest. For, as matters now stand, Mr. Breckenridge, with his pro-slavery platform, must get all or nearly all of the Southern States, but none of the Northern ones, and between him and Mr. Lincoln the latter must be elected. But Mr. Douglas must now step in with a view to get a few northern states, so as to defeat Lincoln's election by the people, and thus throw the election into the House of Representatives where, with a little manipulation of the American states of Maryland, Tennessee, and North Carolina, Mr. Breckenridge can be elected, as all the other slave states are in his favor, and California and Oregon, with their present delegation, may be relied upon for him.

If Mr. Breckenridge is not elected by the House, no one will be, and Joe Lane, who will be made Vice-President by the Senate, will then become President, and it is known that, being a Northern dough-face, his pro-slaveryism commends him equally with Mr. Breckenridge to Mr. Douglas.

Everybody must see that the only effect, therefore, of Mr. Douglas running, must be to divert votes from Lincoln, so as to effect the election of Breckenridge by the House, or of Lane by the Senate to the presidency.

And were he in earnest in his pretended opposition to them, his natural course would be, as he knows he cannot be elected himself, to withdraw from the contest and allow them to be defeated by Lincoln, when seeing the miscarriage of the pro-slavery creed the Breckenridge party might learn, through adversity, to conform to his— Douglas's—pretended standard, and support it as the only alternative of success in another contest. Such would be our advice to Mr. Douglas were we his friend, and wished to save him from utter and irretrievable mortification and disgrace.

But it is evident any calamity to himself is of less importance than to the idol of his affections —the pro-slavery cause; and sink deep as he must, he will never despair of raising thereby Breckenridge or Lane to the presidency. This he expected to do of his own strength, but finding it unlikely that he would carry a State, by which to defeat Lincoln, now he turns to his natural allies, in the pro-slavery work—the American party—for help. Hence the Union of the

Douglas and American parties in the state of New York, to carry that state against Lincoln, and, as we have shown, with no other view than to raise Breckenridge or Lane to the presidency—an object evidently desirable to both these parties. Thus, affecting love for the foreigner, and a desire to extend his rights to the new territories, Mr. Douglas would marshal the Irish and German hosts to his standard merely to march them over to subserve their natural and avowed enemies, the pro-slavery and native American party. We have heard the Irish accused of being led by their passions, and blinded easily by priests and demagogues, so as to be brought to kiss the rod uplifted for their affliction, and thus defeat measures otherwise effective for their amelioration. Will you justify this charge, and now plunge with Douglas into the pool of self-generated slime in which he delights to wallow, and inbreeding there the infection of the Douglas-Bell democracy, bear with you, ever after, that brand of self pollution, which shall render you not only unworthy of sympathy, but objects of abhorrence to those who now seek your own, and our national elevation? Or will you unite with us as co-laborers to strengthen those hands, which, we are confident, are soon to become invested with this office of our national elevation and redemption from its present humiliation and disgrace before the enlightened world?

To the Americans of the Hunt, Brooks & Co. school we make no appeal—such we know to be *constitutional* aristocrats. Envenomed at the loss of power their own Whig party had for sustaining an oligarchy, they actually see, in the aristocracy founded on property in "niggers," a still lingering ray of hope for their futile schemes, to which they will cling with all the malignity and heartless infatuation of their natures. But those who four years ago believed Americanism meant something else than slavery, we invite to the ways of pleasantness and paths of peace, along which, with the cause of humanity, we intend to bear ABRAHAM LINCOLN amid the chorus of our emancipated Nation.

September 11, 1860.

IX.

FITNESS FOR THE PRESIDENCY.

"Is he capable, is he faithful, is he true to the Constitution?" were the tests for office laid down by the great apostle of liberal statesmanship—Thomas Jefferson.

We propose to apply these tests to the candidates for the presidency now before the people.

To possess intelligence, so as to discriminate between right and wrong, and integrity to embrace and adhere to what is right, should seem to include all the considerations necessary to qualify a person for any trust or responsibility; but in view of constitutional obligations this is not enough, and requires the third test of being true to the Constitution. This requirement laid down by Jefferson was found to be not gratuitous by his own political experience. He and the elder Adams were respectively at the head of opposing parties, and while he did not approve the policy of his opponent, which had an illiberal and an aristocratic tendency, violative of the spirit, if not the letter, of our Constitution, he did not impute to him a want of either intelligence or integrity, for it was possible with Adams, as with many minds, both then and now, of the highest order and greatest purity, to regard certain measures of aristocracy, or inequality, necessary to the safety of a State;—a privileged party identified with the safety of a State, and dependent upon its prosperity, who are set to watch over and control those whose labor and industry constitute this prosperity, but whose virtues are assumed to be so low as to unfit them for self-control, and render them mischievous without the restraints imposed by an upper class. This is the present position of many earnest, and we doubt not honest advocates of slavery; and we are aware how hard our opponents now and in times past have striven to establish this principle in our free States.

Mr. Jefferson assumed the opposite of this as his own political creed, and as the true spirit of our Constitution; and the happy effects of his glorious triumph may be taken as the index to the results we confidently anticipate as the issue to the struggle now impending.

In considering Mr. Breckenridge upon the Jeffersonian standard, we find essentially necessary the third point: "Is he true to the Constitution?"

We do not need to examine the two first points to find exceptions: he may be capable, he may be faithful; or, in other words, he may be intelligent and honest, but we thoroughly scorn and revolt at his assumption that our Constitution carries slavery into the territories, and requires Congressional protection there. In this he is *not true to the Constitution*.

Mr. Bell, as a pro-slavery man, is in the same attitude, and technically liable to the same objections. To this he adds the policy of opposing the migration and settlement of foreigners in our country, so as to prevent, as far as possible, the rapid settlement of the territories by free laborers.

Our Declaration of Independence denounces King George III. that "He has endeavored to prevent the population of these States: for that purpose obstructing the laws of naturalization of foreigners," which is precisely the attitude of Mr. Bell towards our territories. When we are ready to renounce the principles of the Declaration of Independence, give up this glorious charter of freedom, and return to the rule of some

George III. of England, then, and then only, will we greet Mr. Bell, his associates, and New York confederates as true, not to our Constitution, but to some obsolete British Constitution, congenial to Native Americanism. Mr. Bell won a good name, and deserved thanks for his manly course in opposing the Missouri Compromise Repeal and the Lecompton Constitution, and we regret he is, by his present course, likely to forfeit the esteem in which he has been held by the public—evincing, indeed, questionable integrity in joining the Douglas party, which affects to despise the American party. But, as mentioned before by us, this is but a trick by which to get the foreign vote, through Douglas, to subserve the southern interest.

To Mr. Douglas our test is so obviously inapplicable, that we turn with loathing and disgust from the attempt. When language has the use Richelieu ascribed to it, of being the means of disguising our thoughts, then will the terms capable, faithful, and true to the Constitution have their ironical application to Mr. Douglas.

Degrade him from the chairmanship of the Senate Committee on Territories—give him a spurious nomination for the Presidency and a sham support—anything his Southern masters may require, and he is happy, so long as thereby he can serve them; no position too false, no humiliation too deep for this labor of love:

> "Look down—your head begins to swim,
> Still deeper yet—that pleases him,
> If he can yet shout 'nigger.'"

It only remains to consider our test in reference to Mr. Lincoln. That he has capacity is seen in the fact, that from an humble, if not obscure position, he has risen to the auspicious attitude he now holds, having in the course of this advancement been placed in many important positions of trust and responsibility, and, as we said some time since, the capacity and fidelity evinced on these occasions secured to him so much confidence and affection, that his friends persisted tenaciously and successfully in his nomination for the Presidency.

In the canvas of Illinois for the Senatorship, he offered to discuss the issues between himself and Mr. Douglas, before the people, to which Mr. Douglas relying upon his usual arrogance and impudence, rather than upon force of argument, assented, and they commenced the work of stumping the State together, but had not gone far when Mr. Lincoln's conservatism and candor confounded the false accusations made by Douglas of sectionalism, and won him great popularity with the people. Thereafter Mr. Douglas refused to meet him in discussion. Upon this discussion, Mr. Benjamin—pro-slavery from Louisiana—remarked, that it evinced sentiments which commended Mr. Lincoln to him over Douglas. The objection raised to Mr. Lincoln and his party is, that they are sectional; and Mr. Douglas, Mr. Filmore, and others, at the North, clamor that he is not conciliatory enough towards slaveholders. Yet both these horror-struck alarmists, before becoming demoralized by a morbid malice and a mania for office were as much sectional as he; both then supported the Wilmot proviso, and said hard things against slavery. Mr. Filmore, now a pro-slavery Bell man, in 1838 said he opposed the admission of Texas as a slave State, the slave trade between the States, and was in favor of abolishing slavery in the District of Columbia. Mr. Lincoln's crime is, that he will not stultify his integrity to play the demagogue. He at this time opposed the passage, by the Illinois Legislature, of certain abolition resolutions, and entered his protest upon the journal, " that the promulgation of abolition doctrines tends rather to increase than abate its (slavery's) evils;" that Congress has no power over slavery in the States; that though Congress had power over the matter in the District of Columbia, "that power ought not to be exercised unless at the request of the people of said District." It is this obvious integrity and sense of justice that commends Mr. Lincoln to his friends and conciliates his enemies. He is capable, he is faithful, and these views show that he is not amenable to the constitutional objections raised against him.

In being opposed to the extension of slavery to the new territories, he is in entire concurrence with the sentiment of the framers of the Constitution, who sought to free the Government from all complicity with slavery or any religious creed. They did so, and Mr. Lincoln, in following them, *is true to the Constitution.*

To a private life of purity, he adds a public character of unspotted integrity and of consistency, and possessing highly practical abilities, we have in Abraham Lincoln a man of associations, character, and habits eminently fitted for the Presidency.

For purposes of State policy our National Executive is invested with great power, both of direct authority and indirectly through his patronage. This has been totally prostituted to the slave interest, with all the moral influence, happily now small, that could be forced into this service.

"The oppressor's wrong, the proud man's contumely, the pangs of despised love, the law's delay (and perversion), the insolence of office, and the spurns that patient merit, of the unworthy, takes," have all had their office in this pro-slavery work, till the corruptions of power on the one hand, and the debasement of servile men on the other, call aloud in agonizing tones, from rock, tree, hill, vale, and plain, and in impetuous echoes resound through the skies, with the demand for a reform, conspicuous of which the time and the man are at hand.

Sept. 22, 1860

X.

THE SECRET OF IT.

The causes of our national revolution, which separated us from the British Government, and which was formally initiated in our Declaration of Independence, in which these causes are so pathetically and eloquently recited, were understood to consist in grievances too intolerable to be borne by men unwilling to be slaves, and to meet these grievances our forefathers of that day, under a sense of their own wrongs, rose to a height of moral grandeur, seemingly above men, and with lips of fire boldly proclaimed the inalienable rights of man, for which, with hearts of steel, they strove in the ensuing desperate, protracted, but triumphant struggle.

The lofty sentiments with which they were inspired, the heroism with which they were sustained, the sacrifices and pains they endured, and the glorious objects they accomplished, in effecting our independence, and the establishment of our Government, have all been exhaustless themes of our gratitude, for the inestimable favors thus secured to us.

With such sacred appreciation have these favors been regarded, that the ark of the covenant—our system of Government—by which they have been transmitted to us has, till lately, been regarded as the *summum bonum* of our race, the lightest disaffection for which, or indifference, aroused our deepest abhorrence and scorn for the calloused susceptibilities that could find outside of it a compensating good, adequate to the sufferings its loss or serious injury must impose.

In contrast to this, we now find disunion of our Government, and disaffection for its priceless liberties, announced with pompous arrogance, as popular sentiments, and as the alternative of not having the national Government administered to the advancement of the institution of slavery.

To an observer of current events, the secret is not that slave owners want more slaves, or slave States, as a means of making more secure and profitable this species of property; for, upon examination, there is not a feature wanting on this head, which could be supplied by such means. The institution carries in itself the elements of deterioration and weakness to those who tolerate it, and has been at all times so characterized, and most pathetically so, by enlightened statesmen who are familiar with it. These, the graphic and prophetic effects of it, depicted by the immortal Jefferson, should alone prove the word sufficient to wise men who would take heed how they hear. But it is the infatuation of the times, and the unscrupulous selfishness of demagogues, that words of wisdom and suggestions of prudence—the fruits of bitter experience—are scouted as the mantling mist of stagnant fogyism, till misapprehension, perversion, and folly have brought us to the present state of absurd wrangling rather than dangerous antagonism.

This state of deterioration and weakness, which is the inevitable concomitant of slavery, has naturally enough awakened alarm with those who tolerate it, for their own safety, and for that of the institution itself. The slave insurrection of 1832, showed their apprehensions well grounded, and the generous guarantees of support, both from the government, through the army and navy, and that volunteered from the North, gave every needed assurance of sympathy for the South, and earnest devotion to our institutions. Happy if the South had seen and met these things in their true spirit! But now start up uneasy politicians, who, Calhoun and Douglas-like, traffic on the gullibility of the people, and assume supernatural powers to foresee direful visions, portending disaster to their darling pet of slavery, to which they affect such a devotion, overriding all other considerations, as to evince the sure qualifications for office.

This scheme succeeded so well, that no man could get to Congress or any other office, at the South, upon any other basis, and at once the hue and cry of "niggerism" is started, as the effective evidence of fealty to a deluded constituency.

Upon this ground Southern men were insisted upon for the Presidency, as security on the one hand against unfavorable executive action towards slavery, and on the other, against executive patronage adverse to its interests. So uniform was Southern sentiment in these respects as to form in the main but one party, and therefore between the nearly equally divided Whig and Democratic parties North, that one was sure of political ascendency which should be found congenial to Southern sentiment. It is easily seen that in an earnest struggle a party had great inducements therefore to court this party of unanimous Southern sentiment, and in this effort both parties strove hard, but the Democratic party succeeded, by trimming party sails, and decking party leaders, to suit their fastidious Southern allies. So patent was this scheme of success to party leaders, that they of the North had only to sacrifice much of their party interests and principles, that by so doing, they pandered to Southern demands so as to secure an undivided support from that quarter.

Ever since this policy was initiated by Calhoun, in behalf of the South, tricky political hucksters, North, have been playing at this game—Mr. Van Buren proclaiming himself a Northern man with Southern principles, so necessary were his southern proclivities to attainment of office.

And when, at times, Northern men become aroused to this imposition, and evince a disposition to revolt at it, the sacred ties and devotion to the Union, to which we alluded above, have no binding force for the South, but our Northern ears are dinned by our political scavengers and patent right Union saviours, with the dangers of disunion, and rhapsodies upon the value of the Union, its cost, and the consequences of its loss, till satisfied it can only be saved, and our political disorders cured by their superior elixirpharmacy. In this way, for some time past, small men and political adventurers have gained position only to disgrace it, and render its patronage and power subservient to the wishes of Southern men, who taking advantage of our susceptible devotion to the Union, have only to threaten us with disunion to raise an army of ready apology office-seekers, to sway us with their sophistries to the necessity of yielding. The Douglas and Bell men North, under their respective leaders, Douglas and Filmore, are now in this condition, whining vagaries and unmeaning misgivings about the sectionalism of the Lincoln men, in order to coerce them into the support of measures revolting to them. Mr. Douglas affects a show of independence, and thereby has subjected himself to the charge of sectionalism by his late Lecompton opposition, but this was a necessity to save some little force North, without which a united South could not save him.

The secret, therefore, of the matter is, that upon a clamor for disunion on the part of the South, Northern men and parties, for sake of office and place, pander to this clamor, to the monopoly, by the South, of the patronage of the Government, and the swaying of executive power in its behalf; and the eternal cry of " nigger" is but the hollow pretence for this clamor.

How well they have succeeded we have lately mentioned in part, and it is evident by the unblushing effrontery with which this trick is now pursued, but with an unscrupulous selfishness sure to defeat its own ends; and thus, aside from the auspices of the occasion, we have a prophetic indication of the return, at last, to the true policy of our Government.

Sept. 29, 1860.

XI.

OUR GRIEVANCES.

THE present prospect of the election to the Presidency of Abraham Lincoln again raises the cry of 1856 from the South against the election of a Republican President, that such an event will justify the Southern or slave States in separating from the Northern or free States, and that, as a duty to their own rights and self-respect, they are determined to do it. In other words, the proposition literally stands, if the North, goaded by the arrogance of the South, backed by the subserviency of the Government power to its purposes, dares to assert its constitutional right of voting for and electing a Republican President, this shall constitute a grievance too intolerable to be borne, and disunion must follow. A fawning Pierce, sunk in truculency, figuratively emasculates his person of manhood and his office of virtue, a blear-eyed old hypocrite now occupying the White House, whose visual obliquity corresponds to that of his moral sentiments, falsifies his oath of office, his promises and obligations, in order to comply with the demands of the pro-slavery power, to which the North is required to submit, and tremblingly refrain from daring once to express opposition, on pain of disunion, with all the rage, revenge, hate, blood, thunder, dust, sword and destruction, to say nothing of smoke and gas, which shall overwhelm us as by magic from the wrath of the South.

What grievances cause all this uproar, and what their remedies, we earnestly inquire. Complaint is made that the people of the North will not give up slaves who escape from slavery and take refuge amongst them. Will disunion remedy this? Will a Southern Confederacy have less dissatisfied slaves, or more power to silence these longings for freedom, and keep out those who excite this longing? The Southern States possess all power now over these matters. But says the South, you are under constitutional obligations to give up fugitive slaves, and as you will not do it, we will save our self-respect and dignity by refusing a voluntary union with such faithless associates. Suppose this true, and a just cause for disunion, the question arises, Why is the election of Lincoln to determine this period for the vindication of a right long since due the South? For it is not easy to see how a few more votes, by which Lincoln may be elected, are to change Northern sentiment on this question—nor indeed are more votes wanted, comparatively—for without the frauds in Illinois and Pennsylvania, at the last Presidential election, Fremont would have been elected. But according to admissions, this ground for disunion now exists, and has for a long time existed, and therefore the election of Lincoln can in no way aggravate this provocation.

On this ground, disunion should have been under way before this time. Thus far our argument admits there are grounds of complaint upon this head; but this we deny. In the earlier history of our Government, some rare instances of opposition to the recapture of fugitive slaves occurred, but no resistance. Not till after 1832, which dates the momentous era of slavery excitement, did resistance arise, and an examination into the facts of the case will show about as many beams in the eyes of our Southern brethren, as there are motes of which they complain in those of our Northern people.

This was the notorious period of those slave

insurrections of the secession nullification schemes of Calhoun, and his dogma of equal political power between the slave and non-slaveholding States. At this time several innocent persons from the North were seized and executed by mobs, for supposed abolition sentiments, and colored citizens of Northern States were, upon arriving at the South, seized and imprisoned.

Judge Hoar was sent to South Carolina to prosecute there, before the United States Courts, the rights of the citizens of Massachusetts, but was forced to leave the State. No Government power here interposed to enforce constitutional rights. Here is a direct and open violation of the constitutional provision that " the citizens of each State shall be entitled to all the privileges and immunities of citizens in the several States," and the courts, provided to enforce constitutional rights, are forcibly deterred from this discharge of their duties. Such discourtesies and want of faith, under the national compact, aroused more or less indignation at the North, and thereupon uprose the abolition organizations, which before had no existence, and which, upon aggravations of the occasion, assumed a strength of number and violence of temper which required the stern efforts of conservative men to successfully oppose. Now, for a series of years, were occasional acts of resistance to the execution of the Fugitive Slave Law, and though no more than due, by way of retaliation, upon the South for a want of fulfilment of constitutional obligations to the rights of Northern citizens, it was not countenanced by any effective or uniform sentiment at the North, and when complaint was made by the South, our Congress-men admitted grounds for it, and announced readiness to adopt the needful remedies, and at once allowed the Southern members to form the present Fugitive Slave Bill of 1850 in the most severe terms, justifying objections made to it, that it gave means to kidnap, and through fraud and violence, force off into slavery free colored persons of the North. This has been done, and notwithstanding this revolting feature, the North acquiesced in this and other measures of 1850, as a final settlement of the slavery question, and the attempts afterwards to capture fugitive slaves were eminently successful. The election of Franklin Pierce followed in 1852, upon the basis of a firm adherence to the compromises of 1850, and never, since the origin of the party were abolitionists, so weak and unpopular. It was a matter of notoriety that their conventions, in the spring of Mr. Pierce's inauguration, had little attendance and no enthusiasm, and the party was dying out for want of countenance. In this state of quietude, returning confidence and fraternal feeling, is sprung upon us that infamous breach of good faith and act of national demoralization, for which its ill-advised and unscrupulous author, now seeking support for the Presidency, deserves the unalterable execration of his race. The wanton repeal of the Missouri Compromise unavoidably aroused rage, indignation, and distrust, which were soon manifest at the North by an indifference to adhere longer to any obligations on the slavery question towards those who utterly disregarded theirs; and if, for some time, fugitive slaves could not be recaptured, the South has only itself to blame for having unnecessarily aggravated this state of things.

The Missouri Compromise averted disunion, and averting or abrogating it, restored disunion or the right of it in the opinion of many at the North. It was this revolutionary spirit that caused so much resistance to the recapture of Burns, in Boston, and upon the ground of revolution, as justifiable, for we recognise the right of revolution, but not otherwise; for, if we are to form a part of the Union, deriving our advantages from its existence, name, and power, we must fulfil our obligations to it, and therefore, as the North was not disposed to dissolve the Union on account of the repeal of the Missouri Compromise, it had no right to withhold its duties under constitutional guarantees—a political apothegm we commend to the South at this time. Let us now view this question in connexion with its effects upon slavery.

Slaves have, for a long time, been rising in value, and this, too, during the cry of a want of security, from Northern disregard of obligations, which would secure it. Property so insecure, as these alarmists would have us believe, would hardly rise thus in value. Moreover it is the far Southern States, where slaves are most secure, and where there can be no complaint about the execution of the Fugitive Slave Law that clamor most about disunion, and not the border slave States, where, if anywhere, slaves escape to the free States. Maryland, Virginia, Kentucky, and Missouri are not disunion States, nor do all the boasts of fiery fulsome fanatics hold out inducements to them to become so. All this hobby about the security of the "nigger" is therefore but a pretext, while the possession of Government offices, and the control of Government power in behalf of the slave interest, are, as we have before stated, the real motives to these pretended grievances.

Oct. 13, 1860.

XII.

DISUNION.

UNDER the heading of "our grievances" we considered the main grievance complained of by the South, as the cause of disunion, and in considering further grievances we adopt, for our present heading, the consequence threatened, as the main object of our attentions.

Our last article showed the aversion, on the part of the people of the North, to the execution of the Fugitive Slave Law, to have been provoked by the aggravations of the South, in doing violence to innocent persons from the North, and under an affectation of fear for the security of slaves, imprisoning, forcing off with many indignities, and executing with mob violence her citizens; refusing to allow the United States Courts to discharge their constitutional duties, and culminating in falseness to her plighted faith by the repeal of the Missouri Compromise. Pursuing thus the suicidal course of provoking enemies towards an institution that needs, for its perpetuity, no little zeal exerted to conciliate friends for it. If our Northern people are implicated in any interference with slavery in the South, we raise no objections to the severe measures of repression the Southern people may adopt, and this has recently been evinced by the uniform acquiescence, at the North, in the treatment adopted towards John Brown and his party in their Harper's Ferry invasion. False and silly is the hue and cry against the whole North for this, as was also the assumption of Virginia's pompous Governor that he possessed facts showing complicity therein of the leading men of the North.

Upon the rights of Congress to exclude slavery from the territories, we, of the Republican party, are on the strong ground that Congress has repeatedly asserted and exercised this right, and that, even putting this exercise in abeyance, as in the Kansas-Nebraska Bill, to which the South was committed in the repeal of the Missouri Compromise, and allowing the people of the territories to express their unbiased will, without fraud or violence, we shall obtain practically our wishes, for, in our enlightened age, the institution of slavery will not be adopted as a matter of choice. But now, under Southern demands, we must overturn our time-honored policy, to interpose by Congress and establish slavery against the will of the people in the territories, upon the alternative of a separation, which, with characteristic blindness, must leave the Southern Confederacy without an inch of territory to extend slavery over.

The tariff can no longer be a Southern hobby. The policy of free trade, so far as consistent with tariff for such revenues as are needed to meet the expenses of the Government, is our pretent practice substantially, and undoubtedly our true policy.

These bugaboo screeches, about the calamity to the country of a Republican President, would have us believe that our President is invested with such absolute authority, that he can arbitrarily exercise it, at the behests of party, and impose such intolerable oppressions, that armed resistance is the only alternative of ignoble submission. Surely, if this is our state, we gained little by our revolution and separation from England, and our forefathers made a sad botch of our Constitution, in not providing against these evils. But this is not so; our forefathers adopted every precaution that the terms of language admit, and it is our painful reflection these terms, both in letter and in spirit, have had their only violation in behalf of the pro-slavery interest.

Some grounds of alarm might justly exist if a Republican President should usurp the unauthorized powers against slavery that have been assumed by the present and preceding administration in its favor, and against which, and further subserviency to the South by our sycophantic Presidents, we are told the North has no right of complaint.

The great and growing power of executive patronage, already beyond the anticipations of the founders of our Government, and capable of sustaining a corrupt party policy, to some extent, against the wishes of the people, is a subject worthy of serious attention with a view to measures of restriction. It is, indeed, against these gross, base assumptions and abuses of executive power that the Republican party has arisen, and however provoked to retaliation, we pledge our party to constitutional and legal measures. And these measures, let us notify our Southern brethren, not by way of threat but of warning, we intend to enforce. As our brave Ohio Senator (Mr. Wade) said, " we submitted to the repeal of the Missouri Compromise and remained in the Union in disgrace, not because we were weak and needed it for support, but because we were strong, and could bear the indignity, under the consciousness of strength available, in due time, to redress our wrongs, and restrain refractory members from fanatical suicide." We endured the Union, under oppression, because of our constitutional right of peaceful redress, and in doing so carry with us the power to bind it, in which we illustrate a principle which it will be our duty to enforce, that in going into an election of Government officers—which to our Government is the peaceful way of correcting abuses—we commit ourselves to the moral obligation to abide the result, and we have no disposition to commit nor to tolerate a falseness and treachery that will not.

From our Northern doughfaces, who tell us the South must have its way or the Union is not safe, we turn with loathing, and leave them to the ignominious oblivion to which their pusillanimity reduced them. As well say to the highwayman, "We pay you tribute and will shield you from punishment if we may pass on in peace;" or to the ruffian who despoils our homes of peace and virtue, "we yield because we want no difficulty with you." To such we say—we desire not your assistance, we fear not your opposition, but we sicken with ineffable shame and disgust that

American mothers ever nourished such unworthy sons.

Our conclusion is, that the North shall fulfil its obligations on the one hand, and refuse a slavish submission to extravagant demands on the other, and that in this the South and the whole country have respectively the only grounds for safety and prosperity. The recent State elections give us the glorious promise that Mr. Lincoln will be our next President, and we pledge him to fulfil his constitutional obligations, but to withhold the executive powers from longer pandering to morbid appetites and disastrous measures.

October 20, 1860.

XIII.

OUR POLITICAL SUMMARY.

It is a consideration of great consolation, and one that, as man improves in his understanding, gives hope of an ultimately high destiny for him, that in all matters of faith and purpose, whether initiated by political or religious associations, there is an assumed integrity of motive, and a decent respect is paid to virtue by affecting a conformity to her dictates. Even in the outrageous measures of the pro-slavery party in our country, operating through their servile tools of the present and past administrations of the general Government, to overturn the dictates of common sense and the experience of past ages, there has been the assumption, however bold and startling, that slavery was the natural and healthful state of society, contributing to its refinement and elevation so much that we must accept it as a social and political blessing. Upon this basis when mankind shall no longer be subject to misrepresentation, and diverted with specious delusions and plausible sophistries, he will set out upon the pathway of his highest prosperity and happiness. The progress of the present campaign for the Presidency gives a hopeful indication of an earnest search for this pathway, or one at least that may save him from the serious blunders committed in following the blind leaders of the Democracy. It is our purpose to point out this path, and encourage our fellow-men to pursue it, and we here recur to the considerations that govern us, to the end that we may confirm in it those of the true faith, and point out the dangers of our heretical opponents who depart from it.

Without alluding to the festering corruptions engendered by slavery in a community which tolerates it, we have opposed its extension into our territories because of its injurious effects upon the free laborer, and consequent diminution of the productions of labor. An appeal is made to prejudice against color, and to the offensive attitude of the abolitionists to charge us with being negro worshippers, Black Republicans, Abolitionists, &c. But with a consistency characteristic of the emanations of malice, we are told that the slaveholders are the true friends of the negro, and by their system they are elevating the black race. The Kamschatkaian would tell us to give up our work-oxen, and use dogs in their place, and thus improve the race of dogs; a morbid snaketamer would have us adopt snakes and lizards for domestic pets, because we thus improve their breed. To this we answer, we are not concerned with improving the black race, nor the breed of dogs and reptiles, any further than such improvement may contribute to the welfare and advancement of our own race—our cause is the white man, and not the negro nor the lower animals. We are told that the welfare of the whites at the South is advanced by slave labor and their wealth of late increased. We admit that the South has shared the great prosperity of our country for years past, but not a proportional prosperity to that at the North. They snarl, "Let us alone; that is our concern not yours, and we will acquiesce in all the evils that slavery may entail upon us." Very well, we say, let us alone too. You may nurse a viper and get stung by it, but we protest that you shall not obtrude your viper upon us, against our will, nor require us to sustain you with the substance it is devouring from you. This you have been doing through the machinery of government, but we propose to modify the workings of this machine. But, says the South, if you won't let the operations of the machine inure to our benefit exclusively, we will stop it, and turn upon you the innumerable and never-ending plagues of our offended wrath. We answer it is our purpose to operate the machine according to its original construction, putting in full play all its component parts and checking any eccentricities that might interrupt the harmony and success of its movements. This mission we commit to the Republican party, and, awaiting their execution of this trust, we set ourselves at rest upon the final issue.

October 27, 1860.

XIV.

A WORD TO THE BRETHREN.

To those who, prompted by an integrity of purpose, possess the intelligence to determine and resolution to pursue the proper objects of our national well-being, we would address a few words in confidence upon impending events. Inspired with a confidence in the ultimate prevalence of almighty truth, party ties, personal affections, and promises of reward have not restrained the manifestations of your noble impulses, nor have fruitless labors, disappointment and defeat dismayed and subdued you.

In the enjoyment of a conscious rectitude, you have a higher reward than any wages of compliance with the demands of the pro-slavery Democracy can afford. Under these sentiments you unavoidably sprang into existence as a party, upon the iniquitous repeal of the Missouri Compromise and the unscrupulous measures of the Pierce Administration to establish slavery in

Kansas. So strong were your numbers there was no doubt that the popular voice of all or nearly all the northern States was on your side, and but for the villanous frauds of your opponents in Illinois, Indiana, and Pennsylvania, your presidential candidate (Mr. Fremont) would have been declared (as in fact he was) duly elected.

In the meantime, under the Buchanan dynasty, you have met a more dogged and shameless opposition than that of the Pierce Administration, and though the name of James Buchanan is justly held in universal contempt, it is difficult to see that it has become so other than in his persistent subserviency to the pro-slavery cause.

In the mean time your policy, both local, in Kansas, and national, in Congress, has substantially triumphed. You have rid yourselves of border-ruffian rule, and established the freedom of Kansas and this great commonwealth of Republicanism. Challenged to this field, you have struggled against the minions of slave oligarchy and the executive power, and, spite of privations and sacrifices, have won a victory, which, in its consequences, may bear comparison with the most signal triumphs in behalf of humanity, and should enrol you upon the roll of fame as the greatest benefactors of your race and nation, and transmit to an admiring and grateful posterity, the record of your heroic virtues.

Alike creditably to Gov. Seward and just to you, did he, in his Lawrence speech, bow before you in reverential acknowledgment of greater services done by you to the cause he had so much at heart, than by any other people. In vain are Governors, Judges, and other Federal appointments made to oppose you. However, prompted by hate of you, and subserviency to the appointing power, they dare no longer trifle with an injured and exasperated people. In Congress your opposition to the establishment of slavery in Kansas, the Lecompton Constitution, the addition of Cuba to increase the pro-slavery power, the opening of the slave trade, and the venality of government officers, has had a gratifying triumph in the face of Executive opposition. And though this opposition defeated your beneficent homestead measure, you have forced upon your opponents in the Senate an acceptance of its principles. So doubly armed are you in this just quarrel, that your enemies, so far from resisting you, are forced to assist in doing the drudgery of your campaign. Your principles therefore, through their own inherent virtues, have had a practical triumph, though the power and patronage of the Government have been in the hands of your opponents, and used with every possible effect against you. You have labored hard, but successfully, and if, by the chances of the coming election, the candidates of your party do not succeed, you can well labor on and wait to behold the confusion and disgrace of your designing opponents, however vainly you must regret the misfortunes of the ignorant and weak who lend support to the very hands that bind them.

Kansas by treachery, fraud, and violence, had been opened to slavery; you sprang to save her, to save yourselves and the north from the disgrace of a craven spirit, that would allow the soil of Kansas, once consecrated to freedom by a sacred compact, to be tamely submitted to the cold embraces of the taskmasters of slavery. Bleak were her then wintry plains, repulsive, savage, and murderous the ruffians with whom you had to contend, and portentous the frowning, opposing power of government; but you hesitated not at them—sufferings, sacrifices, and defeats could not deter you from your purpose. You turned in distress to those you supposed your natural allies and friends in the States. Your vain cry was met with rebuke, that your opposition to the arrogant demands of the South must break up the Union, as submission is the only way to preserve it;

and denunciations, as fanatical "Kansas Shriekers," were the response to your appeal from those constitutional cowards, in whose behalf you were fighting, and who crown their baseness by assisting to foist upon you a new and still more oppressive administration of the government.

You struggled on with a zeal proportioned to the increasing opposition, and you have nobly triumphed. It is impossible you can again be placed under so many adverse circumstances, and the present indications are, that a returning sanity of our people will soon show a due appreciation of your position, and do you justice. If not, be not discouraged; as we have shown, your candidates may not get office and power, but your principles will have a practical success with the people, and your opponents will be placed in awkward confusion with their own blindness and folly,

> "Then bear on, though thy repining eye
> See worthless men exalted high,
> And modest merit sink forlorn
> In cold neglect and cruel scorn.
> If disappointment fills the cup,
> Undaunted nobly drink it up;
> Truth will prevail and justice show
> Her tardy honors, sure, but slow:
>   Bear on, bear bravely on.'

This you will do, and if only to encounter hereafter reverses and opposition, you will know well how to deal with them, and find a satisfactory reward in the conscious rectitude of your conduct.

You are told, if Lincoln is elected, you have to encounter a catalogue of woes, from the disunion of the South from the North and a bloody civil war. You are not to be frightened by what must be regarded as an idle threat, nor will you be unprepared if it should not prove idle. Your Kansas struggle will prove to have been a good school, and the result of it an ominous indication of what may be expected in an issue, where so many circumstances, heretofore in favor of the South, must now be turned against her.

This, the last number of our paper before the election, and, as we hope, triumph of our party in the nation, makes these considerations appropriate to this occasion, and, in submitting them, we join with our illustrious patron of the cause of freedom in Kansas, and "bow in profound reverence before you, as we have never done to any other people —we salute you with gratitude and affection."

November 8, 1860.

XV.

REPUBLICAN REFLECTIONS.

The object of government is security against wrong, whether arising from our private or public relationship. It is the duty of government to guarantee to all its subjects protection from injustice and fraud, and at the same time redress the grievances of society, and punish the aggressions of lawless violence.

When a government fails either from impotence or want of inclination to secure the rights and meet the equitable demands of society, it ceases to command the respect, veneration, and adherence of all freemen.

In a society favored with the wide diffusion of general information, the increased facilities of commercial and social intercourse, and the ameliorating influences of free institutions, the necessity of a powerful government and strict surveillance is obviated. A prompt and ready execution of the laws, and vindication of justice is nevertheless an evidence of a just and efficient government, and promotive of the happiness and welbeing of mankind.

The policy pursued by the last two administrations towards this Territory will brand them in the eyes of a discriminating nation as weak, hypocritical, and false, while the impartial word of history will stamp them with its black broad seal of reprobation and condemnation.

The history of Kansas will remain a foul blot on the annals of liberty, and condemn to everlasting infamy the vile hordes of pro-slavery ruffians who, in 1855, with armed violence, and impending force, polluted the virgin soil of this, Freedom's fair heritage, invaded the polls, and struck down the rights and liberties of freeborn Americans, and sought to establish and perpetuate a reign of tyranny, oppression, and wrong; while the administrations of Pierce and Buchanan, if they did not aid and abet, at least connived at these demonstrations of lawless violence, will excite in the bosoms of all law-abiding men a perpetual loathing and disgust.

The leading object of the Pierce and Buchanan dynasties has been to establish the institution of slavery on a broad, national, and permanent basis, and secure and perpetuate the ascendency in the Federal government, of an element of power, which, like a rapacious oligarchy, is sapping the foundations and absorbing the liberties of the laboring classes.

Those peculiar leading measures of the Pierce administration, the repeal of the Missouri Compromise, and the passage of the Kansas-Nebraska Bill, the authorship of which Mr. Douglas makes his boast, and which have yielded him the greater portion of his fame, and which will mark him in the eyes of posterity as a political intriguer, reveal, when viewed in the light of collateral facts and circumstances, a broad conspiracy, and deep-laid plot to betray, in all the territories, the constitutional rights of freedom.

Excluding altogether from our consideration the public avowals of leading Southern statesmen, who have controlled the Government during the last eight years, and interpreting the spirit and design of the Federal administration through the policy which it has persistently and assiduously pursued towards its pioneer citizens, we are led inevitably to this conclusion.

How else can we explain the manifest distaste and strenuous opposition of the administration, in 1856, to a public investigation of the outrages perpetrated in Kansas? The greedy haste with which a pro-slavery and obnoxious constitution was sought to be forced on a protesting and indignant people, and the repeated refusal by a Democratic senate to admit Kansas with a constitution, the embodiment of her enlightened choice, and which, harmonizing with the Declaration of Independence, guarantees freedom to all?

These acts have been scrutinized by the eye of a discriminating nation; and the spirit of a fearful retribution has swept over the party under whose protecting shadow the reign of tyranny and violence in Kansas has been continued, and torn, and rent, and wrecked and precipitated it to ruin, while liberty in her mild glory and serene radiance prepares to mount the throne of the nation. There may she live, and reign, and sway this vast Empire till the world shall end, and time's last note be heard sounding upon the trumpet of eternal doom.

Nov. 10, 1860.

XVI.

OUR TRIUMPH.

Thanks to the success of Republicanism in Kansas, we have telegraphs and presses to which we have been indebted for the early intelligence of the results of the election, which reached us, at this point, about forty-eight hours from the closing of the polls on election day.

Our last week's issue announced the happy tidings to our rejoicing readers, that Abraham Lincoln and Hannibal Hamlin were, on the 6th inst., elected to the respective positions of President and Vice-President of these United States, to which they had been nominated by the Republican party in Convention at Chicago.

An undeviating purpose—obstinate as it was cruel—to subvert the framework of our national policy, and substitute therefor a gloomy pile, upon which, and tottering beneath its load, the hopes of humanity and the happiness of our people were to be sacrificed as a holocaust to slavery, has been resolutely pursued, for the last six years on the part of the advocates of slavery. Arrogant and domineering in spirit, and, through the powers of the general government, oppressive in manners towards the people of the North, they claimed the right of rule, to which cowardly commerce and timeserving office-seeking politicians lent themselves, and to perpetuate this rule, every resort that art could devise, and fraud and force effect, has been adopted to this end. Oppressed through these long years of lonely darkness, the cohorts of freedom have struggled on to reach, at last, the daylight of deliverance which now dawns upon them. Thank you from the depth of our heart, beloved brethren of the North. We bow at your feet in humble acknowledgment of our gratitude due you for asserting your own and our manhood, unswayed by bribes, unintimidated by threats.

We now rise to our proper level, and in catching the first rays of light and breath of deliverance, our impulse is one of unbounded joy, and we have hardly been able to do else than indulge our feelings and manifestations of delight.

But we must reflect that, as we take our new position, we are involved in new duties and responsibilities, and it becomes us, thus early, to reflect upon the proper discharge of them, to the end that we may justify our promises and the hopes of our race, and avoid the errors and follies which have swept the Democracy from existence, and made the name of it, as identified with the corrupt Buchanan, the seceding Breckenridge, and the compact-violating Douglas, a byword for all that is deceitful and unjust.

OUR POLICY.

Our policy should therefore be, to administer this government with equal justice and honor to all parties of the country, and not necessarily, as has been done for many years, in behalf of a class whose impudence and presumption correspond to their idleness, incapacity, and poverty, and who, upon the capital of a few "niggers" at their command, claim all refinement and gentility of society, and a monopoly of the lucrative offices under the government. Pampered and spoiled by these indulgences, it is this class that has brought us our present troubles, to remedy which the Republican party has arisen; and of course it follows, that to continue the same policy would defeat the purposes of the party, and still further exasperate the evils we seek to cure. What most we have wanted is a president who would do justice to the North, without being swayed by a senseless and false clamor that, by so doing, he would fail of justice to the South. So sensitive would some of our conciliatory presidents have been, that to avoid the charge of being partial to the North, they would have neglected to do it justice, in order to pacify the exacting and capricious South. This was the apprehension concerning Mr. Seward, and this feature of his character had much to do towards the defeat of his nomination. Nor would we indulge in any spirit of retaliation towards the South, in revenge for the gross injustice we have suffered at her hands. Our new President, we are confident, understands his mission in these respects.

He should administer the Government himself, in accordance with the theory of our Government, and call the heads of the respective departments to their positions, to assist him, not govern him, correcting in this respect the awkward position of Mr. Buchanan, in which the heads of the different departments exercise their functions, and give orders in their own name, irrespective of the President, as though an independent power, therein, existed in them.

The Secretary of the Treasury sends in his

report, and urges upon Congress a tariff policy the very reverse of that recommended by the President. We fancy Secretary Cobb would have cut a sorry figure, as a cabinet minister of General Jackson, in opposing his views of state policy.

Mr. Secretary Floyd indicates, irrespective of any known views of the President, that the matter of Disunion is in his hands, and that he is uncertain what is his duty, and how far he shall use the force of the army to prevent secession of Southern states, just as though this was exclusively his office, and not that of the President. Mr. President Lincoln, the power is yours alone—use it; the responsibility yours—discharge it; and the reward due, either of praise or blame, shall be yours. Do not, Buchanan-like, timidly shift upon your irresponsible secretaries a responsibility which devolves upon you alone.

SLAVERY.

Not to be disturbed where it now exists, nor to be abolished in the District of Columbia without the wishes of the people, and then by moderate degrees.

The Fugitive Slave Law to be enforced in good faith; the present law should not be changed to impair its efficiency in it.

Slavery is *not* extended by our Constitution over the territories. On the contrary, they are free in the absence of law establishing slavery, and no such law should be made till a territory becomes a state, when she can, if it be the unbiased will of her people—that will being expressed without force or fraud—provide for slavery, and should not be refused admission to the Union on this account. Such we believe to be our true policy, and, so far as we understand, the views of our President elect.

DISUNION,

however, threatens to become a great question for the solution of our new President and his party.

If a state avails herself of the advantages of the Union, she should share the responsibilities of it. She grows in prosperity under the ægis of our laws and our protection; shall she escape her share of our adversities, arising from war or debts unavoidably incurred? Upon every principle of moral obligation, no state can of right withdraw from the Union, without the consent of the others, but by revolution.

We prefer discreet measures of restraint and coercion on such an occasion; but we doubt the probability of any necessity for them.

XVI.

PROPOSED AMENDMENTS TO THE CONSTITUTION.

In his late message to Congress, the President, after an elaborate discussion of the present threatening aspect of affairs in the southern states, and the absence in Congress of the constitutional power to compel the continued allegiance of the states to the General Government, proposes to pacify the slave states, and perpetuate the Union by a fresh sacrifice on the altar of slavery. Mr. Buchanan would have the North bow its knee, and worship again the imperious God of negro slavery. He would have another exhibition of craven submission to the exacting demands of ruthless oppression and despotic violence.

The sway, and almost absolute control by the South of the Federal Government, has been broken, and because two or three little states fret, and fume, and kick like spoiled children, Mr. Buchanan is alarmed. "The grandest temple which has ever been dedicated to human freedom—which has been consecrated by the blood of our fathers, by the glories of the past and the hopes of the future—is about being destroyed and the nation enshrouded in a long night of leaden despotism." "The hopes of the friends of freedom throughout the world are to suffer annihilation, while our example will be quoted as a proof of the failure of the theory of self-government." To all these threatening and alarming calamities Mr. Buchanan has discovered a remedy. He would convert this, the grandest temple of human freedom, to a huge charnel-house of human bondage. He would meet and sustain the hopes of the friends of freedom, by fastening more securely on the nation the growing curse of oppression. He proposes to demonstrate the practicability of self-government by dooming an unoffensive race to hopeless, unending slavery, and reducing the majority of a free nation to a meek, tame, and unqualifying submission to the iniquitous exactions of an imperious oligarchy.

Mr. Buchanan uniting in himself more sagacity and patriotism than was possessed by the whole band of our Revolutionary sires, has detected a radical defect in the Constitution, a breach in the fundamental law of the nation, which he proposes to patch over with slavery. Slavery is discovered to be the cohesive force which will bind these States in fraternal union, while the irrepressible conflict must cease, since freedom is to be pushed out, and slavery shoved in.

We are to have a *final* settlement of this question, by a new construction of the Constitution, giving an "express recognition of the right of property in slaves in the States where it now exists, or may hereafter exist." Also "the duty of protecting this right in all the common territory throughout their territorial existence, and until they shall be admitted as States into the Union, with or without slavery as their Constitution may prescribe; together with a like recognition of the rights of the master to his slave, who has escaped from one state to another, to be restored and delivered up to him, and the validity of the Fugitive Slave Law, enacted for that purpose, accompanied with declaration that all state laws impairing or decreasing this right are violations of the Constitution, and consequently null."

It might be pertinent to suggest to our venerable President, that there have been several *final* settlements of this vexed question already. The Jeffersonian Ordinance of 1784 was intended to be final, and while it received at the time the entire support of the South the North was satisfied. The Missouri Compromise was the next final settlement; but this not meeting the entire demands of the South, Congress, in 1852, to allay agitation, and save the Union, enacted the Fugitive Slave Law. The fourth final settlement was commenced by Mr. Douglas, and the Popular Sovereignty dodge was to banish slavery agitation from the Halls of Congress. The lameness of this settlement having been made apparent on a short trial, the Supreme Court steps in and makes a final disposition of the whole matter.

We can but commend the sagacity of the hero of this new final settlement. Mr. Buchanan's proposition covers the whole ground; he would even anticipate the future wants of the slave power. "All the South has ever contended for, is to be let alone and permitted to manage their domestic institutions in their own way as sovereign states." Then why, Mr. Buchanan, botch the noble character of our liberties with the foul features of slavery?

December 1, 1860.

LETTER I.

CAMP, NEAR MOUND CITY, KANSAS, *December* 16, 1860.

You may wonder that I have not earlier fulfilled my promise to write you upon the troubles in this region of country, but were you to listen, as I have done, to the numerously conflicting statements, of great and equal credibility, on the respective sides, you would find all the delay I have observed necessary to an approximate appreciation of the facts and merits involved in pending issues. I say approximate, for I do not believe any stranger to the past scenes and the relations involved can ever understand them in their true features. I had not been here an hour when all the occurrences were made known to me about as well as they are now, but on inquiring for the reasons of them I was answered, by a gentleman of apparently just views, that this was a complex matter, and doubtless had some, though not direct, foundation in the embittered animosities engendered four years ago, when, in imitation of, and consequent upon the national breach of good faith, in the repeal of the Missouri Compromise, every breach of human right and moral obligation was committed to force slavery upon Kansas.

The occurrences which have occupied so much public attention consist, mainly, of the execution (by hanging) of two men, Hinds and Scott, and the shooting of two others,—Moore and Bishop. Hinds lived near the state line on the Big Osage (or Marais Des Cygnes), and was charged with kidnapping negroes, one of whom was a free man, and carrying them over into Missouri and selling them as slaves, and with having shot at Dr. Jennison of this town, with intent to kill—the Dr. having been fired at twice on his way home at night, by some one concealed by the roadside. Scott lived some fifteen miles north of here near the mouth of Mound Creek, which empties into the Big Osage, and was charged with having largely participated in the outrages of 1856, and though repeatedly notified to quit the country, he had not done so. Goods taken by him from free-state men in 1856, were said to have been found in his house, when he was hung. Moore was shot upon refusing to give himself up, for having been a leader, and boasting of it, in the hanging, some time ago, of a man by the name of Hugh Carlin. Bishop was shot accidentally in the attempt to arrest Deeds, whose son-in-law he was, and at whose house he was staying. These executions have not been committed by a mob, exasperated by a sudden passion of revenge for some recent outrage, but by a committee of nine or twelve persons appointed for this purpose, and to execute the decree of the people, who have doubtless organized as a secret order, and hold their secret conclaves to determine the destinies of their fellow-men, and the welfare of society. If these things are done for the interests of the community and under its sanction, it is safe to assume that the same measures of redress could be effected by law, and through the forms of law, which is understood to be the most solemn and mature expression of a whole people upon this best system of civil polity, and as such should become the rule of action to every individual, and only through its effective operation can the rights of all be secured, and peace, harmony, and prosperity prevail. Violence may originate with the many, under spontaneous and pure impulses, but will be maintained only by a few depraved natures, who delight in the indulgence and manifestation of their passions, the unchecked effects of which must be, terror and slavish fear on the one hand, and arrogance and indiscretion on the other— breaking up that industry from which virtue and prosperity arise, engendering bitter animosities and brutal resentments, depriving the community, through fear and violence, of its best citizens, till wantonness and rage bear sway, and unlicensed outrage exhausts herself in anarchy and ruin. The people here are so far under the censorship of this order, that they dare not openly differ with it— torments of the inquisition, the terror of the guillotine, the unrelenting rigor of a Cotton Mather, stand sentinels before their lips. The intolerance of the people in the Southern states towards those who favor freedom is here practised, to some extent, towards those who favor slavery, and is excused on the ground of this example, and that having suffered so much from pro-slavery men it is unsafe to tolerate sympathizers with them.

But it is not altogether a question of extending or preventing the extension of slavery, but, to some extent, of abolishing it where it exists, and opposing the execution of the Fugitive Slave Law. Few if any could be found here willing to aid in the return of a fugitive slave, and many of the secret order (of Montgomery and Jennison) would violently resist. It appears our arrival here drove off several blacks, who, in escaping from their masters and coming here, had remained under assurance of protection from recapture, but which protection would doubtless prove unavailing in the presence of troops. Strait-laced, hidebound puritanism, which finds an exclusive and infallible guide in Scripture teachings, here dictates these things irrespective of the fact that the same supple authority, under Southern interpretation, requires as a condition of man's salvation, that he shall either become a master and own a slave, or else he shall have a master, and *become* a slave.

But you will notice I am criticising what are for the most part local prejudices and peculiarities, with which I have nothing to do, nor has the General Government. A violent death here and there is no concern of the General Government, except when perpetrated in violation of her laws; but the deaths here, were in violation of the laws of the territory, and had nothing whatever to do with the United States laws, nor has the General Government any business in the matter, till the Governor reports that he is unable to preserve peace, and makes requisition for assistance. This the governor has not done, nor has he been consulted in the matter. Judge Williams—the Judge of this district—did indeed run away in a fright, and despatch a frightful account, which having been found to be almost entirely false, it is doubtless the business of the Government to withdraw, and leave local troubles to an adjustment by the people concerned. Judge Williams was not disturbed nor threatened, nor were any of the land officers at Fort Scott, nor were public records disturbed. Neither was Missouri invaded nor threatened; nor were troops collected and fortifications raised under Montgomery, with a view to revolutionary measures. Montgomery seems to hold much influence here and has firm adherents and friends, and though doubtless privy to what is here transpiring, his participation in the late executions is uniformly denied by the people here.

Gen. Harney, with Artillery and Dragoons to the number of some 150, left Ft. Leavenworth on the 27th ult, and proceeded to Fort Scott, and we were stopped here, where we arrived on the 5th inst. After using the troops to assist in making some arrests at Fort Scott, the Artillery, under Capt. Barry, joined us here on the 6th, and the Deputy U. S. Marshal—a Mr. Campbell of Fort Scott—was supported in attemps to make arrests here. Montgomery, Jennison, Seaman, and the two Forbeses were sought for at their houses, for the purpose of arresting them, but they were not found. The Artillery were sent back to Fort Leavenworth on the 9th, the Dragoons to Fort Scott on the 10th, and go into quarters there. Gen. Harney left Fort Scott on the 11th for Leavenworth, and we—two Companies 2d Infantry—remain here in tents, with alternate cold, snow (six inches depth of which fell last Thursday night) and drizzling chilly rains, with mud, superlative wretchedness, and disgust ineffable. All this is with a view to help the Marshal to make arrests, and if Montgomery and Jennison do not give themselves up, we have no idea how long we may have to remain. It appears that they are willing to give themselves up to the sheriff of the county, to be tried for offences against the laws of the territory, and in the usual way, but are not willing to be sent over to Fort Scott, and kept in jail there, to be tried there before Judge Williams, sitting upon cases of the United States, with such authority to the Marshal for empannelling a jury, as will include too many Missourians to do justice to a Kansas Free State man.

The present state of affairs cannot be justified. Much may be plausibly urged as a provocation. A suspension, at last, of border invasion and Federal oppression, through corrupt officials, had been followed by a dearth and famine, in the midst of which, the President caused their lands to be offered at public sale, forcing the settler to pay for his land, to secure it against the risk of loss. A suspension, in one instance, for one year, was allowed, I am informed, by permitting a re-filing, and paying again to the Land Offices a filing fee. It seems to me a pertinent inquiry, how, if the President felt it his duty to direct the sale, was it not possible to evade this duty by permitting a re-filing, and why, if not necessary to have them sold, were they so ordered, and this order suspended to give double fees to the Land Officers? Upon the survey of the Miami lands, many persons unexpectedly found themselves upon them, and though the Indians had power to sell, and were anxious to sell, the President would not permit it, and these people were expelled and their improvements lost.

The New York Indian lands were open to settlement, the Indians having their head rights, and had been surveyed, so that, seemingly, no trouble could arise from settling upon them; but in running off the Cherokee neutral lands they were recently run on the New York Indian Lands eight miles, putting the occupants of this strip of eight miles wide, on to the Cherokee lands, and from which they were recently driven, in the midst of distress, and their buildings burned. Captain Sturgis's First Cavalry obtained, as you will remember, some notoriety through the public press in connection with this matter. Long accustomed to regard the troops as their allies in the pro-slavery cause, the Missourians became heroic under their auspices, and on this occasion they waxed furiously valiant, and organized, I am informed, a secret order, called the "Dark-Lantern Order," with a view to renew invasions in Kansas, and reconnoitred with boldness and insolence through this region, with a view to future operations. Just now, and like an opposing and overpowering wave, came in these victims of oppression from the Miami lands and New York Indian lands, joined in spirit of exasperation, if not swelled in numbers by the settlers suffering from the land sales, and considerably augmented both in spirit and numbers by the fugitives from the pro-slavery proscription in Texas. The last pound on the camel's back had long since been placed, and his only chance of life lay in kicking off the additional weights, brought for him to bear. A counter secret organization was formed, with the results so far before us, and it is claimed for this body, that, up to this time, their efforts have been to nip the incipient stages of the onset extensively prepared against them. A project is fondly entertained to erect a slave state out of the Indian territory to the south of Kansas, and to embrace in this new state a portion of the south of Kansas. It is believed the Cherokee lands were run up so high north, and that the Missourians proposed to add an additional strip by conquest. The bringing in of troops from the remoter posts, and the unnecessary ordering of them here, without a demand by the Governor, are explained upon this supposition. All this may have its due force in the way of provocation, but it does not justify systematic violence, in the redress of wrong, when that redress can be effected through the forms of law. Nor is a persistent determination to encourage the escape of slaves and to resist the Fugitive Slave Law, to be justified, and this determination, I regret to say, has a potent though not a preponderating sway here. It may be observed, that the toleration by the General Government of Southern contempt of its authority, justifies a belief in an already virtual disunion, and the victim of oppression by pro-slavery men and measures, feels himself no longer under constitutional restraint upon measures of redress. But this is revolution, and no more commendable than that which is appealed to as an excuse.

LETTER II.

FORT SCOTT, KANSAS, *January* 19, 1861.

I AM in doubt whether you will care to hear again from me, as I have nothing of interest to report upon the late troubles which seem to be now suspended, and you are now abundantly occupied with the solemn events (not to say farces) now enacting with a view to the dissolution of our Government. I am glad to see some signs of sanity and spirit, at last, in our imbecile "old public functionary," and that he can bring his mind to comprehend that, as President of the United States, he is invested with powers and involved with responsibilities to meet this great disunion question in the only light which, as a legal, moral and physical question, it exhibits, and that is, in the light of revolt and treason. The right of independent sovereignty in the respective states may appeal to the pride of a people, and some may vainly suppose it to have existed, but this is obviously inconsistent with the existence of a separate Government, formed by the Union of these States. For then our Union would be but a voluntary league, in which no Government, as such, could exist—the efficacy of our Constitution all along misapprehended, and the operations of our Government to this time a blunder.

In fact, I may say no State of our Union ever has been independent, as a separate sovereign power. Certainly the original thirteen States were not, for until the declaration of their independence of Great Britain they were, of course, colonies to that Government; and that declaration of itself was not made in behalf of separate States, but, in its own language, "in the name and by the authority of the good people of these colonies," and goes on to declare "these *United* Colonies are, and of right ought to be free," &c., so that their very act of throwing off colonial allegiance was by means of a Government formed from a union of the Colonists. And immediately thereafter was formed the articles of Confederation, which were not formed under any idea of separate sovereignties in the respective States, but with a view to the best form of Gvernment for all the States, as a Union. And these articles of Confederation expressly and repeatedly provide, that this Union "shall be perpetual.". Years of experience proved the articles of Confederation to have defects which called for a remedy, and for this purpose the present Constitution was adopted, with the avowed purpose, as its preamble states, "to form a more perfect Union," and none of the conditions of its perpetuity, provided for in the articles of Confederation, were abrogated by this new Constitution. And this Constitution, by its own provisions, and their adoption by the respective States as such is the Constitution of those states. For the language of paragraph second, Art. 13th is, "This Constitution and the laws of the United States which shall be made in pursuance thereof; and all treaties made, or which shall be made, under the authority of the United States, shall be the supreme law of the land; and the Judges in every state be bound thereby, anything in the Constitution or laws of any state to the contrary notwithstanding."

The law, in terms and by clear inference, is conclusive against the existence of independent sovereignty in the respective states, and I have indicated, above, that the thirteen original states have not had for any one a separate existence as a sovereign power. Of course it will not be claimed that the new states, admitted into the

Union have had. Texas exercised such power, and was so recognised by most civilized nations, as a revolted province of Mexico, but Mexico never admitted it, nor was her separation from Mexico effectual till her union with us under our Constitution, which being accepted, became her supreme law, anything in her Constitution or laws to the contrary notwithstanding.

I stop here with the legal question—the moral obligation should have no less force. We all know that South Carolina escaped vassalage to the British Government through our Union, and that she and all other seceding states hold their present high positions through the aid of the Union, and having availed herself of these advantages, through the Union, she cannot absolve herself from her obligations to the Union. Wars have been prosecuted, debts incurred, and conditions entered upon, and must a part of the states, faithful to the Union, meet all the responsibilities without that aid implied in the Union, and as a condition of which their own was pledged? One state, in adopting our Constitution may have made more sacrifices of her existing interests than another state, but she did so upon the right to hold the other state to the obligations she assumed in entering the Union, and as a condition of which the sacrifices were made. Much might be said of the sentiments of our forefathers, the history of those times, and of the logic of the question, to enforce these views, and from which we find no other conclusion that the laws and morals of this disunion movements concur to denounce it as revolt, and to be dealt with as the best interests of our Government require.

If such a modification of the Constitution could be effected, as to allow the slave states to withdraw, this would seem to afford a peaceful solution to the trouble, but only seemingly, for difficulties would soon arise to involve the opposing states in war. But were it not for the certainty of this war, I would not object to this sort of settlement, for then the North would be at once rid of all responsibility for slavery, and of this eternal unhappy wrangling over it. But this mode is impracticable, and the only thing left is for the Government, through its constitutionally organized means, to exercise its authority over the seceding states, in a discreet and conciliatory manner, till the present unfounded excitement subsides. Of course the present acts of violence should be met and arrested, but more with a view to indicate the right of authority, than to redress a grievance.

But I did not sit down to write homilies upon our Government, or to indicate precepts which every schoolboy in our country should know and make his rule of thought and action, but I have been unavoidably drawn into it by the theme, and this must be my excuse.

So far as I know there are no items of local interest to mention. Montgomery, so far as I can learn, is not disposed to give the South the benefit of his example in their revolutionary schemes, and is therefore reserved, for the present, upon the execution of any he may have contemplated. But in all seriousness, if we are to have civil war on this slavery matter, this abolition element will prove a powerful and effective one in the prosecution of it. I would pledge Montgomery, with ten thousand followers in the slave states, to equal the exploits of Xenophon and his ten thousand Greeks. Mark this, and time shall show.

APPENDIX.

APPENDIX.

REMINISCENCES OF GENERAL LYON.

As everything connected with this fallen hero possesses a historic as well as local interest, we may be excused for referring again to his birth-place, and the battle in which he lost his life.

Several accounts have been given of the manner of his death. Dr. G. G. Lyon, his relative and brigade-surgeon, who was with him a moment before and again a moment after he was shot, says that General Lyon had been wounded by a shot in the heel, a shot through the fleshy part of his thigh, and a shot which cut open the back of his head to the skull bone, and was covered with blood, when he saw him riding between the Kansas and Iowa regiments to lead them to the charge. He begged him to retire to the rear and have his wounds dressed. General Lyon replied, "No—these are nothing," went forward, and was killed by a Minié ball through the breast and out at his back, which severed the aorta, or principal blood-vessel of the heart. He fell into the arms of Lehman, his body-servant, and said, "*Lehman, I am killed; take care of my body,*" and instantly expired. Those were his last and only words.

In private life, in the camp, by the fireside, or anywhere with his friends off duty, General Lyon was one of the most mild, genial, and pleasant of men. Said one of his intimate friends, "You wouldn't suppose he ever would get angry, or be roused to excitement." His favorite attitude was standing and stroking or picking his long sandy beard. But on his splendid horse, at the head of his little army, he was literally "a tower of strength." His form straightened up two inches taller; his eye dilated and blazed with excitement, and his commands were given in trumpet tones that were heard and *obeyed*, through all the deafening din of battle, and he was incapable of fear.

The battle of Wilson's Creek was a most desperate fight. About three thousand five hundred was the number of our effective troops, who went out to contend with twenty-three thousand of the rebel army. The numbers of both sides were pretty accurately known to both armies, by their spies. To lie still at Springfield would be fatal, to go forward could be no worse—the reinforcements so long and impatiently wished for, so imperatively needed, did not arrive. General Lyon determined to give battle, not expecting to be victorious, but hoping to cripple the enemy sufficiently to cover his retreat. Another reason, not without weight, was to show the rebels that he could *fight*, before he turned his back on them.

The result is before the world. They fought like Leonidas and his Greeks—they fairly and completely whipped a force of six times their own number, but suffered so terribly they were unable to pursue. *Could* they have had but *two* fresh regiments, say Lyon's officers, " we should have chased them into Arkansas" and ended the war in Missouri. Regiments had asked to be permitted to go to Lyon's aid, weeks before, but were withheld. There is a bitter feeling against the Secretary of War in consequence.

In the course of the battle, Captain Plummer—an experienced officer of the regular army, who is modest as he is brave—was stationed in a large cornfield, with four companies of regulars, where he was atacked in front and in flank by three regiments of rebels—nearly three thousand men. Said Lyon, when Plummer's position was reported to him, "He's lost." But Captain Plummer and his brave band faced the deadly crossfire, and *cut their way through*, coming out with only ten men to his largest company. Captain Plummer received a Minié ball in his hip at the commencement of the attack, but maintained his seat on his horse, and the lead of his men, till they were out of present danger—he then fainted and fell, badly wounded. "It was hard," said Captain P., relating this scene, "to see men that had been with me in all sorts of danger for twenty years, fall wounded, begging for help, and be unable to give them even a drink of water; and to be obliged to leave them, and see some of them bayoneted on the spot by the rebels."

Then, after Captain P. and his surviving soldiers had cut through, and the three thousand rebels crowded the cornfield, Captain Totten's artillery opened on them with terrible effect. Dr. Lyon was near enough to see them distinctly with his glass. The round shot ploughed bloody furrows through the thick ranks, and shell and shrapnell carried death on every hand. Just here occurred the following extraordinary incident, witnessed by Dr. Lyon, just before the enemy retreated:

A tall rebel soldier waved a large and costly secession flag defiantly, when a cannon ball struck him to the earth, dead. A second soldier instantly picked up the prostrate flag, and waved it again—a second cannon ball shattered his body. A third soldier raised and waved the flag, and a third cannon ball crashed into his breast and he fell dead. Yet a *fourth* time was the flag raised—the soldier waved it, and turned to climb over the fence with it into the woods. As he stood astride the fence a moment, balancing to keep the heavy flag upright, a *fourth* cannon ball struck him in the side, *cutting him completely in two*, so that one half of his body fell one side of the fence and the other half the other side, while the flag itself lodged on the fence, and was captured a few moments afterwards by our troops. Our troops captured three rebel flags, but lost none.

The body of General Lyon was laid out in state at the camp, at the close of this bloody day, and not an officer or private but shed bitter tears as they gazed on their dead General, almost idolized by every man of them from the highest to the lowest. He was buried on the farm of Colonel John S. Phelps, a native of Windham county, Connecticut, and for many years a member of Congress from Missouri. He is a strong Union man, and is now raising a regiment for the United States army, while the rebels have seized his property.

General Lyon was never married, it being a frequently expressed opinion of his that a soldier ought not to encumber himself with a family. It is stated that he left a will leaving all his property, worth some $30,000, to his country, to which he has already given his life. His sword, chapeau, and commission were given by his friends to the state of his nativity.

Another incident is worthy of record in this connexion, also related to us by Dr. Lyon. We refer to the daring and desperate charge of Lieutenant Sullivan and fifteen of the United States cavalry, at the cattle of Dug Spring, in which General Lyon was engaged. Lieutenant Sullivan, in the course of the battle, suddenly found himself faced by a full regiment of rebels. With a sudden impulse he loudly shouted: "All brave men follow me!" and dashed forwards like lightning, fifteen men following. With one jump they were out of sight, in the midst of the rebel ranks; then their sabres were seen flashing and slashing, and their pistols heard cracking. For an instant the centre of the mass was seen to heave and sway, then the rebels wavered and broke, actually driven by *sixteen* men, and the little band emerged from the turmoil with four killed and six wounded. And, what is most remarkable, Lieutenant Sullivan came out with *five* balls in his own body and *thirteen* in his horse, none of which proved fatal! Both man and horse are now nearly sound again, and, says the brave Lieutenant, "There isn't money enough in the United States to buy that horse!"—*Hartford Evening Press.*

OBSEQUIES OF GENERAL LYON.

The body of General Lyon, which was temporarily interred, as we have already mentioned, on the farm of the Hon. J. S. Phelps, about three miles from the battle-field at Wilson's Creek, was shortly afterwards exhumed by his relatives, under a flag of truce, and transported to St. Louis.

The turn-out of the military at St. Louis (says the funeral-editor of *The Herald*, to whom we are indebted for what follows), was immense. Stores and dwelling houses were draped in mourning, and the entire city seemed to bewail the fall of this gallant soldier as a national calamity.

In Cincinnati the obsequies were likewise observed by the citizens and soldiery, and upon the arrival of the body it was placed in Smith and Nixon's Hall, and there laid in state, guarded by the military.

In Pittsburg, the corpse was received by several companies of the Home Guard, and escorted to the depôt, Major Conant, the Aide-de-Camp of the late General, and commander of the escort, declining any more extensive demonstration.

The military of Philadelphia paid marked respect to the memory of the illustrious deceased, detachments of the First Artillery Home Guard acting as guard of honor, and the Second Infantry of the line, Colonel Dare, escorting the body to the railroad depôt.

THE ARRIVAL IN NEW YORK.

The steamboat Richard Stockton, running in connexion with the Camden and Amboy Railroad, arrived at the foot of Courtlandt Street at about half-past two o'clock, on the afternoon of the 31st of August. The flags of the vessel were at half-mast, as well as some of the shipping in the vicinity. At the ferry the Third Company National Guard, Seventh Regiment, New York State Militia, having been detailed as an escort by Colonel Lefferts, was drawn up in line, and presented arms when the body, carried by the guard detailed by Major General Fremont to accompany it, passed through. A large number of citizens was also present at the pier to witness the arrival of the corpse.

THE ESCORT OF THE REMAINS.

The following military and civic gentlemen composed the escort:—

Major H. A. Conant, Quartermaster of General Lyon's division; Captain George P. Edgar, of General Fremont's staff; Dr. G. G. Lyon, of the

Missouri Brigade, a cousin of the deceased; Captain J. B. Plummer, of the United States Army, who was wounded in the battle of Wilson's Creek, who is accompanied by his wife; Lieutenant E. J. Clark and eight privates of the Missouri Home Reserve Corps in uniform; Danfield Knowlton, Esq., of this city; J. B. Haslet, of Webster, Massachusetts, brother-in-law of deceased; Mr. P. McQuillan, of the Cincinnati *Gazette*, and James H. Brown, of the Cincinnati *Times*.

THE MARCH TO THE CITY HALL.

After the appropriate ceremonies of taking charge of the coffin by the company of National Guard troops, the line of march to the City Hall was taken up in the following order:—Company C, Seventh regiment, with arms reversed; section of police of Twenty-seventh precinct; Drum Corps of Seventh regiment, with muffled drums. Undertaker and hearse, drawn by four horses, caparisoned with sable plumes and crape, and escorted on either side by the officers and privates of the Third Missouri Home Reserve Corps; Officers and friends of the deceased followed the hearse in carriages.

THE BODY AT THE GOVERNOR'S ROOM.

At an early hour in the morning, Mr. Roome, the keeper of the City Hall, received orders to prepare the Governor's Room for the reception of the corpse, where it is to lie in state until its removal to Eastford, Connecticut. He accordingly draped the large chamber inside and outside in mourning, and placed the flags on the roof at half-mast. The entrance to the City Hall was guarded by policemen, who kept the crowd at a respectful distance while the body was being carried to the Governor's Room.

When the funeral cortege arrived in front of the Hall, Captain Price drew up his company in line and the coffin was taken from the hearse by the Missouri soldiers accompanying the remains, and carried to their designated place. The undertaker had already placed pedestals in the centre of the room, upon which the corpse was deposited. Beyond the company of the Seventh Regiment and the members of the Common Council, no one was permitted to enter the room. Sergeant Legett posted his guard immediately, which are relieved every two hours.

THE BURIAL CASE CONTAINING THE REMAINS.

The wooden box in which the remains of the deceased were placed was considerably shattered while on the journey to New York; consequently the body was put into a metallic coffin, painted to represent rosewood.

In the centre of the coffin was fastened a silver plate, bearing the following inscription:

"General Nathaniel Lyon, died August 10, 1861, aged 42 years."

The burial case was bedecked with the American flag. At the head lay the chapeau of the late general, in the centre a wreath of evergreens and *immortelles*, and at the feet the sword which was grasped in General Lyon's hand while leading his gallant troops. The escort accompanying the remains from St. Louis withdrew, as soon as Captain Price took the body in charge, to their quarters at the Metropolitan hotel.

The remains of General Lyon lay three days in state, at the City Hall. On the 2d of September, free access was allowed all persons to view the coffin from nine o'clock A.M., until one o'clock P.M., and during that time upwards of fifteen thousand persons visited the Governor's Room, where the remains have reposed since their arrival in this city on Saturday last. A body of police carefully guarded the entrance to the room, and none were admitted but those who really seemed to understand the scene on which they were about to gaze. Company C, of the Seventh Regiment, Captain Price, were detached as a guard of honor, to keep watch over the body, and two soldiers stood at the head and two at the foot of the coffin during the day. The stream of visitors continued during the entire time allotted for the reception, and one by one the citizens were admitted, who slowly walked around the coffin and made their departure through another door at the extreme end of the room.

The whole proceedings were conducted with that solemnity and good taste which were due to the memory of the departed soldier, and the deeds which have made his name famous in the annals of his glorious profession. Each visitor looked as though he or she felt with a true force, the peculiar circumstances which led to the untimely death of the brave Lyon. Although the coffin was not uncovered during the day, and no curious eyes could gaze upon the sacred features of the dead, yet all seemed imbued with the same melancholy and holiness of feeling which are sure to be harrowed up when confronting, face to face, the grim monster death. All knew that Nathaniel Lyon lay within the narrow limits of his last couch, wrapped in his winding-sheet, with that eagle eye, which was wont to gaze upon so many scenes of bloodshed, closed for ever; with that arm, which so often dealt the death-blow to the enemies of his country, now palsied in death; with that heart, which pulsated so warmly with patriotic emotion, now stilled for ever; and with that tongue, which at Wilson's Creek rung out the notes of encouragement to his charging soldiers, now unable to utter a syllable. These were reflections enough to make all feel sad. Ay, there lay General Nathaniel Lyon, clothed in the robes of the grave, but surrounded by those whose hearts beat aloud in commiseration for his hasty death. Every one felt that he died the noblest death known to humanity. They pictured in their mind's eye, the stirring scene where he fell from his horse and yielded up the dearest boon that humanity can boast of—life—in defence of his country and her honor. They thought, in the distance, they recognised that tall form seated upon a horse, with his eye lit up with the valor of his soul, as with hat in hand he cheered on the men of the Union to charge the enemy. There he sat as proud as any mortal can be, for his position recognises it. He cared not for the storm of iron hail that swept its terrible course above and around him, for the red, white and blue fluttered before his vision and obstructed all other objects. But see, his last hour has come. The General falls from his horse struck by a bullet from the enemy; his countrymen surround him; those eyes are glazed in death; one glance towards the enemy's lines, a last towards heaven, and Nathaniel Lyon yields up his spirit to his Creator.

A number of officers of our volunteer and militia regiments also thronged the room during the day, and hundreds of ladies were among the civilians who gazed upon the coffin. It was a refreshing sight to see tender-hearted women weeping as they passed through—a just tribute to the memory of the soldier. On the coffin were the sword and hat of deceased, together with a quantity of flowers strewn upon the lid. The flag under which the general fought and fell was wound around the head of the coffin, attached to which was a piece of white paper, with the following inscription:

TO THE LION-HEARTED GEN. NATHANIEL LYON.

    Thy name is immortal;
    Thy battles are o'er;
    Sleep, sleep, calmly sleep,
    On thy dear native shore.

NEW YORK, Sept. 2, 1861.

The poetry was written evidently by a lady, and was placed upon the coffin during the day.

THE FUNERAL PROCESSION.

It was not until shortly after three o'clock that the military began to form in the Park for the funeral procession. The Park was filled by a large crowd, who conducted themselves with that decorum and silence which befitted the place and the occasion. The Seventh Regiment were drawn up in line opposite the Hall, and presented a splendid appearance, dressed in white pantaloons, grey coats, and full dress hats. Silence reigned amid the vast crowd, and no jocose word or rowdy expression disturbed the solemnity of the hour. At four o'clock the coffin was borne from the Governor's Room by the Missouri volunteers, who escorted the remains home, and placed upon the hearse, drawn by four grey horses, which was in readiness to receive them. The procession then filed into Broadway, as follows:—Detachment of the Fourth Regiment Artillery, with four guns; Companies B and C Third Regiment Hussars, two hundred men; Grafula's Band, thirty pieces; Seventh Regiment (National Guard), seven hundred strong; Hearse; Missouri escort and Co. C, Seventh Regiment, on both sides; officers of the Sixty-ninth, Sixth, Eleventh, and other regiments; carriages containing members of the Common Council.

Broadway was crowded on each side with people, but the occasion was in itself a more peculiar one than any which our citizens have been called upon to participate in for some time. No enthusiasm could be exhibited, no cheering or waving of handkerchiefs, none of the wild excitement which has been the leading feature of our great thoroughfare for the past four months. All was sombre and still. The multitude were aware of the duty which they owed the dead soldier, and respect, sympathy, and devotedness were plainly portrayed on every feature. The people lined the sidewalks on either side, while the windows and piazzas were equally well filled with ladies, who gazed sadly down upon the soul-stirring procession. Nearly every flag upon Broadway, and indeed throughout the whole city, was at half-mast, and several of them draped in mourning. The guns of the artillery detachment which joined in the procession were also draped in mourning, and Broadway never before looked so sombre as it did while the funeral was wending its way to the New Haven Depôt. The Seventh, marching with their arms reversed, headed by a fine band playing the mournful strains of a dead march, lent a good deal of solemn grandeur to the whole scene.

The route of the procession was up Broadway to Fifth Avenue, up Fifth Avenue to Twenty-seventh Street, and up Twenty-seventh Street to the New Haven Railroad Depôt, where the body remained over night, in order to be transported to Connecticut at an early hour the next morning.

The body of General Lyon was removed to Hartford, prior to its interment in the family burying-ground at Eastford. The ovation tendered to the inanimate body of the brave soldier, on the part of the citizens of Hartford, was tremendous, the military and the citizens vieing with each other in the demonstrations of respect towards the dead, and of hospitality to the escort. When the escort arrived at Hartford, it rained as if the gates of Heaven had broken loose; yet, notwithstanding the shower, the parade in all its details was observed, and the remains lay in state at the Capitol, guarded by the City Guard and Light Guard alternately.

A special train was provided to convey the body of General Lyons, his escort from St. Louis, the military of Hartford, consisting of the City Guard, Captain Prentice; the Light Guard, Lieutenant Kiffen commanding, accompanied by Colt's Armory band, and a rifled six-pound field piece. Among the guests on the train were Major General J. T. Pratt, commanding Connecticut State Militia; his Honor Mayor Dinning, of Hartford; ex-Governor Cleveland, Colonel G. S. Burnham, Second Connecticut Volunteers; Captains Gore, Merrills, and Holcomb, of the same regiment. The following gentlemen acted as pallbearers in the procession to the cars on leaving Hartford:—General Pratt, Major Dey, Major Goodwin, General Waterman, Major Leverit Seymour, and David Clark, Esq.

The train carrying the remains and the escort was draped in mourning, and left the depôt about one o'clock, arriving at Willimantic about a quarter past three o'clock. This place being a large manufacturing town, employing numerous hands, chiefly females, was all alive. Not only the actual residents of Willimantic were assembled at the depôt, but from a circuit of thirty miles around, the country folks flocked in to the town to do honor to the remains of the brave deceased, and to behold the mournful scene. American flags, large and small, draped with black borders, were suspended from houses and trees, and the weather even seeming to harmonize with the solemnity of the occasion.

The day was beautifully serene, and not a breath of air wafted those banners hung at half-mast to signalize the grief of the multitude. This being the terminus of the railroad towards Eastford, whither the funeral cortege was wending its way, arrangements previously made for the conveyance of the party escorting the remains were carried into effect. Hundreds of wagons, from a single horse buggy to the cumbrous market wagon drawn by four horses, were pressed into service. Major Dorsett, the Sheriff of Windham county and Postmaster of Eastford, superintended the disposal of the vehicles, and after a great deal of labor, and considerably after four o'clock, the cortege was set in motion. First came the military, then the Missourians in charge of the remains, deposited in a hearse drawn by four jet black horses, which were brought along from Hartford. Next came an immense number of conveyances, carrying the relatives of the deceased, and citizens. The roads were lined with people, young and old, and flags at half-mast were visible at almost every house the cortege passed. The tolling of village church bells added materially to the solemnity of the occasion. To give a correct number of the vehicles in the procession would be a thing next to impossible. Certain it is, however, that they exceeded three hundred.

Eastford, which is sixteen miles distant from Willimantic, but having a somewhat hilly yet not impassable road leading thereto, was reached at about nine o'clock by the head of the procession. About a mile and a half from the town the Light Guard, City Guard, of Hartford, with their band, Mayor Conant and his party, composing the pallbearers and numerous citizens, alighted from their vehicles and formed in procession. On a hill, a short distance to the right from where the cortege commenced to move, was planted the six-pounder, mentioned above as being carried by the Hartford City Guard, which pealed forth minute salutes, while the bells of the churches at Eastford tolled a mournful chime. When the cortege came to within a half or three-quarters of a mile from the town proper, the road, being lined on either side with fine trees, myriads of lights, candles, lanterns, rushes, and every conceivable burning material were ignited to illuminate the path. The people were arrayed on the right and left of the road, the males respectfully doffed their hats, while the females manifested signs of respect and grief otherwise. Nearly all the windows of the houses in town were filled, and especially those fronting the road on which the procession passed. The whole scene was sad and affecting, the band playing the "Dead March in Saul" as the church was reached wherein the body of the illustrious dead was to be deposited until the final burial service, on the next day. The remains were placed on a bier in the Congregational church, which is situated on an eminence, west of the road by which the cortege entered the village, but was reached by a circuitous route, in order to give the townsfolk an opportunity to see the torchlight procession.

The City Guard, in command of Captain Prentice, had the honor of guarding the remains of General Lyon during the night, the watches being set every two hours, and relieved according to the rules of the service. The remainder of the escort were taken care of by the inhabitants, some of whom accommodated no less than fifteen or sixteen persons, and supplied them with comfortable beds. And here it will not be out of place to particularize the genial hospitality of the inhabitants of Eastford, who were only too pressing in forcing their bounty on their guests. To mention any names, and not enumerate the entire inhabitants, would do the latter great injustice; but the writer of this will be pardoned if he pays the compliment of a notice to Rev. C. C.

Adams, the Methodist Episcopal Minister; H. B. Burnham, Esq.; Rev. Mr. Chamberlin, of the Congregational church; Dr. Robbins; Foster Skinner, Esq., and a few others, whose names he could not obtain. To Mr. Burnham our reporter is personally indebted for the courteous and hospitable manner in which he treated him, inasmuch as the only tavern in the town could not possibly accommodate any more than were there already on the arrival of the procession.

Having reached Eastford safely, deposited the coffin and its esteemed remains under a guard at the church, and disposing of the escort quartered comfortably, we will now turn our attention to the flourishing town itself, which, prior to this occurrence, was comparatively unknown in this city, except by those who stood in business connexion with it, or had probably relatives residing there. Otherwise, to the masses it was an unknown spot, and to some it would even have been a difficult task to point it out on the map. Nevertheless, Eastford is not an unimportant town in the wooden nutmeg State, as it will be seen directly.

The site of this place seems to have been selected with an eye to the health of its inhabitants, as well as a romantic location. Surrounded by hills, from which a pure air is wafted, the soil affords the most beautiful wells, which are sunk on an average about twenty feet below the surface. Through the east side of the town flows a somewhat unimportant river, known as "Still River," which is not navigable, but is used extensively for watering cattle. Northward, about half a mile before reaching the town, however, this stream falls a distance of about thirty-five feet, the roar of which is somewhat similar to the Buttermilk Falls at Troy. The water of these falls runs with such rapidity that it would prove invaluable as a power for manufacturing purposes.

Eastford is situated in Windham County, sixteen miles north of Willimantic, and twelve miles south of Southbridge, near which latter place is the State line. Eight miles east of the town is Putnam, a station on the railroad leading to Norwich, Providence, and Boston.

The industrial enterprise of the place consists of the manufacture of woollen and cotton goods, shoe manufactories, tanneries, etc., and likewise of considerable farming interest, the cultivated lands being situated beyond the hills surrounding the town. Windham county is the one that gave the Republicans of Connecticut the majority at the last election for Governor, and to the inhabitants of that borough Governor Buckingham owes his election over his less successful democratic opponent, General Pratt.

In our Revolutionary history the county of Windham has also played a most important *rôle*. Within its borders lived General Israel Putnam, at Pomfred, five miles east of Eastford; the gallant Colonel Knowlton and Hale were born at Ashford; and last, though not least, the lamented, brave, and heroic General Lyon, who offered up his life on the altar of his country's integrity, drew his first breath of life in the romantic little village we here describe Another star in the galaxy of renowned individuals, who is claimed by the people of Eastford as one to "the manner born," is the Hon. Galusha A. Grow, Speaker of the House of Representatives, who is only known as the Hon. Mr. Grow, of Pennsylvania, from the fact of his having resided there almost since his infancy, but is nevertheless a native of the "land of steady habits," and of Eastford.

The population of the town, as shown by the last census, is somewhat over 1200. It also boasts of three churches—a Methodist, a Presbyterian, and a Congregational, and a tavern tolerably well kept, three stores, and very hospitable, generous people. Pretty ladies also abound here. The produce raised hereabout consists mainly of corn and fruit, while hay forms a very important item to the farmer, which pays him a very fair income. Poultry in great numbers is raised by them, mainly for the Boston market, and about the holidays hundreds of tons are sent to this "City of Notions" for home consumption. The Bostonians, by paying a higher price for that luxury than New Yorkers, are preferred, and consequently receive almost the entire stock raised in this neighborhood.

Sickness in the town of Eastford is a thing almost unknown, and although it has a resident physician —a very clever man, Dr. Robbins—if he had to depend upon the cases coming under his care at Eastford he could scarcely earn enough to feed his horse. A Post Office, of which Major Dorsett is the keeper, is also situated here, and a daily mail is received from nearly all parts of the country.

The houses are mostly built of wood; here and there can be seen a structure of brick, or brown granite; but the major portion are constructed with rare architectural beauty, and the vegetable and flower garden invariably grace the front side thereof.

This is about as full a description as can be given of this town, and it can scarcely be credited that such a vast number of people as were assembled there on the day of the obsequies of General Lyon could have found accommodation for themselves or their beasts. Thursday, the 5th of September, dawned with all the brilliancy of an Indian summer morning. The heavy dew soon melted before the rays of a powerful sun, and had it not been the mournful occasion that attracted the vast multitude, the appearance of the town would have likened more a fair on a gigantic scale than the funeral of a brave and honored soldier. As it was, the scene the town presented, even in its mournful aspect, was one of solemn interest, moving the beholder to thoughtfulness, if not to gravity.

Almost from break of day the rattling of wheels and patter of horses' feet were heard coming into town, each vehicle loaded down to its utmost capacity with men, women, and children, the occupants being decked out in their Sunday-go-to-meeting clothes. Huge baskets of provender accompanied the expedition; and, notwithstanding the mournful errand, the good people from the country seemed to be conscious of the fact that one cannot exist upon grief and sympathy even for one day.

The fact of the remains being deposited in the Congregational Church seemed to be known to all comers, inasmuch as soon as the horses and wagons were safely brought in everybody ascended the hill upon which the little church is built, and from six o'clock in the morning until near eleven one continuous stream of people lined the road to the chapel. On the slope of this eminence benches for the accommodation of visitors were erected, while on the edge of the highway, running below the hill of the church, a distance of probably five hundred yards, stood a platform, about forty feet long and twenty feet wide, covered with boards as a protection from the sun.

On the platform were seated the chairman, the orators, representatives of the press, and invited guests. The seats fronting and in the immediate vicinity of the platform were reserved for Mayor Conant and the Missouri escort, as also for the Hartford escort.

Mayor Dorsett, the marshal of the day, assisted by numerous aids, constituted themselves into a police corps, and kept order among the assembled multitude, which, at the hour of opening the exercises, could not have amounted to less than fifteen thousand people.

The platform was occupied by the following distinguished personages:—His Excellency Governor Wm. A. Buckingham, of Connecticut; his Excellency Governor Wm. Sprague, of Rhode Island, and staff, consisting of Colonel Lyman B. Frieze, Colonel Tyron Sprague, Colonel John A. Gardner, Colonel Thomas Harris, Attorney General Walter S. Burgess, and Paymaster General J. C. Knight; Mayor of Providence; Hon. Galusha A. Grow, Speaker of the House of Representatives; Senator Foster, Hon. A. A. Burnham, member of Congress, from the Third District of Connecticut; Major General J. T. Pratt, Connecticut Militia; Brigadier

General Casey, United States Army; General Schouler, of Massachusetts, of Governor Andrew's staff; Colonel J. W. Witherell, do.; R. Montgomery Field, Esq., of the Boston *Post;* C. C. Adams, Paymaster United States Army; Captain Knowlton, First Artillery, United States Army, Instructor at West Point; Hon. Richard Busteed, of New York; Hon. J. B. Colt, of Missouri; his Honor Mayor Deming and Postmaster Cleveland, both of Hartford; Major Warner, of the Third Connecticut Regiment; Colonel Cooley, of the First Connecticut Regiment; Major H. J. Conant, Aide of the late General Lyon; Captain J. B. Plummer, First Infantry, United States Army; Major G. G. Lyon, Brigadier Surgeon to the late General Lyon; Captain G. P. Edgar, General Fremont's staff; Lieutenant E. J. Clark, Third Missouri Reserve Corps, and many other distinguished gentlemen, both military and civic.

At half-past ten ex-Governor Cleveland called the assembly to order, and in a terse and feeling manner stated the occasion of the vast concourse, and begged the audience to pay particular attention to the orators of the day. A chorus of ladies and gentlemen, led by Rufus Weston, chaunted the hymn:

"Hark from the tomb a mournful sound."

After which an impressive prayer was offered up by Rev. Mr. Williams, of Chaplin—who was for ten years pastor of the church, opposite which the ceremonies were conducted—for the deceased, his friends, and the preservation of the country.

Ex-Governor Cleveland introduced Judge Elisha Carpenter, of the Supreme Court, and residing at Killingly, who delivered a lengthy oration on the life, character, rise, and progress of General Nathaniel Lyon, whose history he traced from his birth until his untimely death on the 10th day of August last, while gallantly leading his army. The Hon. Galusha A. Grow followed the Judge in an eloquent strain.

Mr. Grow commenced his address by remarking that "once more he enjoyed the blessing of standing upon his native heath, but he did not expect that it would be upon so solemn and melancholy an occasion. They had assembled at a sad hour; they mourned a nation's loss, and the soil that covers the remains of a Putnam, a Hale and a Knowlton, and shortly a Lyon, has already become sacred to the memory of every patriot." The speaker then illustrated how Martin Luther first incepted the revolution in religion while confined in a dreary dungeon, and how successfully he accomplished it. He then passed on to the period of the discovery of this continent. He continued—"Another period is passed, and on an icy December morning the good old ship May Flower lands her precious cargo on our shores, and a new era begins. But let us skip a century and a new child is born. The Revolution, like a flaming river, whose fires all the water in the world could not quench, is instituted. A Constitution is framed and a great nation declared itself free and independent. We gained the victory then, as also in 1812, and at present we are to see whether that Constitution can be maintained against the corruption and treason hatched by traitors, and in whose defence the noble hero lying yonder, cold and inanimate, sacrificed his life. Nations cannot be punished in the next world, and must be in this. The loss of war comes home to our (your) firesides; lives must be sacrificed, and the affliction of one whom you love and respect is at the present at your door. The speaker continued, that that was the day to sow the soil with the blood of the noble martyrs, from which would spring forth armed heroes to defend that sacred Constitution fought for and obtained by the hearts' blood of our ancestors. While the shores of the Adriatic were desolated with war, leaving its harrowing traces behind, we see with horror the retrograde movement of one of the greatest experiments. A revolution fought three-fourths of a century ago must be fought over again, and what a costly war it was. Yet to gain our liberty, yet costly as it appeared, it was cheap at any price. To maintain the integrity of our

Government such men as General Lyon suffered death; and when the time should come that free Governments cannot be sustained, even at such sacrifices, then we must give up in despair and pronounce republics a failure. But as long as a united people are determined to stand by the Constitution, and a Government—the best and most liberal on the face of the universe, such fears are impossible to be realized. To-day your townsman falls, to-morrow one from a distant State—so it was in the days of 1776—valuable lives were then lost as at present. The flag watered by their blood is now dishonored, and this is done by men born under the shade of the flag of Washington, nurtured by the institutions which were established by our forefathers, and who are acting the parricide to perfection in deliberately trampling under foot the costly and dear-bought victory of freedom. The speaker further said, if four millions of people are competent to overthrow the work of our sires against twenty millions, then it deserves to be a failure, and the sacrifice of many valuable lives, like the one who lies in yonder church, must invoke the very heavens for vengeance on those by whose acts they have been made martyrs. The meeting of the day, Mr. Grow continued, was to pay a tribute of respect to one of the martyrs of the present revolution. The boom of the cannon at Lexington raised an obscure Colonel to the proud leader our forefathers had in General Washington. More such men, who are at this moment in obscurity, will be found to lead on our victorious armies, and bring back our glorious country to her former proud position. Let the bier pass on. Nathaniel Lyon, though slain, will live for ever in the memory of his countrymen. How can a man die a nobler death than by facing the fire for the sake of his country? The very waters will murmur a requiem to his memory. His body is interred in his native soil, his monument is the granite hills, and his headstone a nation's grief. The speaker concluded with the following brilliant sentence:—Fortunate in life, he is doubly fortunate in death. If there be on this earthly sphere a boon and offering heaven holds dear, it is the last libation liberty draws, and the heart that bleeds and breaks in its cause.

Mr. Grow took his seat quietly, and even the solemn occasion could not refrain the audience from giving vent to their plaudits by clapping of hands.

Governor Wm. A. Buckingham was then introduced. In the course of his speech he remarked that Ashford, in the days of the Revolution, gave to the cause of liberty a Knowlton, who fell early, and was lamented by General Washington; and to-day a vast concourse had assembled to pay homage to the remains of another son of Ashford, whose loss a nation mourns. Such men as Putnam, Knowlton, Warren, and a host of others fought for our freedom, a sacred Constitution, and all the blessings we have enjoyed were their handiwork. To maintain its integrity the brave and honored son of Connecticut fell a martyr. Thanking the audience for their attention, and the Chairman for his compliments, Governor Buckingham gave way to the popular Executive and gallant military chieftain—

Wm. Sprague, Governor of Rhode Island. In response to the wishes of the audience he mounted a chair to address them. This was the first time in his life, he said, that he had appeared before an audience in another state; but in order to become more familiar with his neighbors he had pitched his tent among them. He did not come to Eastford to receive honors, but to do honor to the lamented dead. He was proud to avail himself of the privilege to tread upon the native soil of one whose life was sacrificed in the cause of his country. He admonished all to emulate the example of General Lyon in patriotic devotion to his country and her cause. That country was now in danger. All our efforts were necessary to preserve its purity. Even women and children could be of great assistance. Let every youth buckle on his armor and go bravely to the field and do his duty there with patriotic determination. Let our women imitate the example of the women of '76, and the contest will soon be over. The time for words or debate has long since passed, and at the present moment it is not the power of argument, but the power of battalions that is the sinew of war. These are the doctrines I promulgated in my own state, and I take the liberty to breathe them in another. Marshal your forces, stem the tide, and bring back our country to its original purity and glory. Rhode Island will do her duty; Connecticut must not forget her obligation, and when victory again perches upon our banners the states will be closer united than they have been heretofore. The Governor continued for some time in this patriotic strain, and finally gave way to Judge Colt of Missouri.

The Judge spoke of the virtues of the deceased soldier, whom, whilst in St. Louis, he had learned to esteem for his many good qualities. He concluded by saying that if Connecticut had more men like General Lyon in the field, Missouri would not long remain in dread of rebel hordes.

Captain Edgar, of General Fremont's staff, paid a high compliment to the deceased, also to Major Conant; Captain Plummer, of the First United States Infantry—who so signally distinguished himself in the battle where General Lyon lost his life—Lieutenant Clark and the escort of the body from St. Louis.

Major Conant, aide to the deceased commander, was also called upon and made a few appropriate remarks.

Senator Foster was next introduced. He spoke of the valor of General Lyon, and said he deemed it an honor to have the remains of such a patriotic and gallant man repose in his own native soil. General Lyon was a brave man, and the citizens of Eastford should show the country that they are worthy of being his townsmen by enlisting in the cause in which the former lost his life to defend.

Mayor Deming, of Hartford, spoke eloquently for some time, enrapturing his hearers. He also paid the highest compliments to the many good qualities and undaunted heroism of the deceased, eulogizing his acts at the battles of Contreras and Churubusco, where he shed his first blood for his country. In Kansas, Oregon, and Missouri the heroic General has fought bloody battles and distinguished himself. His Honor concluded:—" How sweet and glorious it is to die for one's country and for people's liberty."

The Hon. Richard Busteed, of this city, who was present by invitation, closed the exercises with an eloquent and affecting address—which, for want of room, we are compelled to omit—after which the assemblage dispersed for the purpose of taking some refreshments before proceeding to the burial ground, two and a half miles distant. The speakers and guests were entertained with a bountiful repast by the Committee, Governor Sprague occupying the head of the table, with Governor Buckingham on his right and Major General Pratt on his left. Rev. Mr. Chamberlin said grace before the meal.

The funeral cortege assumed its march about half-past three o'clock in the following order:—

A cavalcade of one hundred and fifty horsemen in command of Colonel Sabine; Tiger Engine Company, No. 7, of Southbridge; Home Guard, of Woodstock; Band; Light Guard, of Hartford; Colt's Army Band; Hearse; City Guards; Pall-Bearers, both sides; Officers of Army and Navy; Principal mourners and relatives of deceased; Citizens on foot, and citizens in carriages.

The procession was at least a mile and a half in length. The pall-bearers were Governor Sprague and Major General Pratt on the right, and Governor Buckingham and Brigadier General Casey on the left. It was generally and favorably remarked how well Governor Buckingham and General Pratt fraternized in behalf of our country, since only a short time has elapsed when these two gentlemen were gladiators in the political arena for gubernatorial honors.

The burial ground, which is located at a village called Phœnixville, two and a half miles distant from Eastford, was not reached until nearly five o'clock. The plot in which the remains were deposited is the family vault, embracing about twenty five feet square, surrounded by four granite pillars, from which iron chains are fastened to serve as a railing. In this lot the deceased members of the Lyon family are interred, among whom are the father and mother of the late General.

The graveyard is small, and lies in a vale surrounded by sloping hills. In the centre thereof weeping willows of great height and beauty serve not only for shadow, but to ornament this homestead of the dead. The hills were thickly dotted with human masses, and the military, forming a hollow square around the fresh made grave, the firemen immediately in the rear, and the people standing and sitting on the sloping hills, altogether formed a scene for a Church or a Kenset to reduce to canvass.

Rev. C. C. Adams, the Methodist minister of Eastford, performed the Methodist Episcopal burial ceremonies; Major Conant, Captain Edgar and the St. Louis escort partially filling up the grave; after which the City Guard, under orders of Captain Prentice, fired a volley of three rounds over the grave, while the band performed a dirge. The spectators then quietly withdrew. The relatives expressed their sincere thanks to the St. Louis escort for their kindness in closely guarding the remains.

The relatives of the late General Lyon consist of

two brothers, John and William, both of whom live in Windham county; Mr. J. B. Hasler, who married a sister of the General, residing at Webster, Massachusetts, and an unmarried sister. The brothers are men of family, and mostly all of their offspring were present on this occasion.

The ceremonies attendant upon the interment of General Lyon will form part of the history as yet unwritten, and the inhabitants of the quiet little town of Eastford will, a long time hence, remember the immense congregation assembled within its precincts to pay the last tribute of respect to the remains of the valiant but unfortunate chieftain. To Major Conant, Captain Plummer, Captain Edgar, Lieutenant Clark and the eight members of the Third Missouri Reserve Corps, the greatest credit is due for their unceasing watchfulness over the corpse entrusted to their charge.

The people having paid just homage to the gallant Lyon, and his own native soil covering his now inanimate body, let us drop a tear to his memory and turn away to brighter scenes, encourage our living heroes to do their duty to their country like the illustrious deceased, and our land will very soon again enjoy the blessings of which rebel traitors endeavored to rob her.

Requiescat in pace.

IN MEMORY OF GEN. LYON.

Enfurl our flag half-mast to-day,
   In sorrow 'mid the clang of war,
Each crimson stripe is turned to gray,
   To black each golden star.

The drooping breeze scarce stirs a fold,
   The birds complain with fettered breath,
The clouds hang sullenly and cold—
   For lo! a hero's death!

From far Missouri's prairie plain,
   The echo of his battle cry
Sounds and recedes, and sounds again
   His life-earned victory.

O, Lyon! on thy martial bier
   The tears of grateful millions flow;
And treason well may shrink and fear
   Its fated overthrow.

For wheresoe'er thy comrades stand,
    To face the traitors, as of yore,
Thy prescient spirit shall command,
    And lead the charge once more.

Then fling our flag mast-high to-day,
    Triumphant 'mid the clang of war,
And death to him who shall betray
    One single stripe or star!

New York Evening Post.

LYON.

Sing, bird, on green Missouri's plain,
    Thy saddest song of sorrow:
Drop tears, Oh clouds, in gentlest rain
    Ye from the winds can borrow;
Breathe out, ye winds, your softest sigh,
    Weep, flowers, in dewy splendor,
For him who knew well how to die,
    But never to surrender.

Uprose serene the August sun
    Upon that day of glory;
Upcurled from musket and from gun
    The war-cloud gray and hoary.
It gathered like a funeral pall,
    Now broken and now blended,
Where rang the bugle's angry call,
    And rank with rank contended.

Four thousand men, as brave and true
    As e'er went forth in daring,
Upon the foe that morning threw
    The strength of their despairing.
They feared not death—men bless the field
    That patriot soldiers die on—
Fair Freedom's cause was sword and shield,
    And at their head was Lyon!

Their leader's troubled soul looked forth
    From eyes of troubled brightness;
Sad soul! the burden of the North
    Had pressed out all its lightness.
He gazed upon the unequal fight,
    His ranks all rent and gory,
And felt the shadows close like night
    Round his career of glory.

"General, come lead us!" loud the cry
    From a brave band was ringing—
"Lead us, and we will stop, or die,
    That battery's awful singing."

He spurred to where his heroes stood,
    Twice wounded—no wound knowing—
The fire of battle in his blood
    And on his forehead glowing.

Oh, cursed for aye that traitor's hand,
    And cursed that aim so deadly,
Which smote the bravest of the land,
    And dyed his bosom redly!—
Serene he lay while past him pressed
    The battle's furious billow,
As calmly as a babe may rest
    Upon its mother's pillow.

So Lyon died! and well may flowers
    His place of burial cover,
For never had this land of ours
    A more devoted lover.
Living, his country was his bride,
    His life he gave her dying;
Life, fortune, love—he naught denied
    To her and to her sighing.

Rest, Patriot, in thy hill-side grave,
    Beside her form who bore thee!
Long may the land thou diedst to save
    Her bannered stars wave o'er thee!
Upon her history's brightest page,
    And on Fame's glowing portal,
She'll write thy grand, heroic rage,
    And grave thy name immortal!

H. P.

Philda. Saturday Post.

www.ingramcontent.com/pod-product-compliance
Lightning Source LLC
Chambersburg PA
CBHW031940230426
43672CB00010B/1994